Essentials of Field Relationships

Qualitative Essentials

Series Editor
Janice Morse, University of Utah

Series Editorial Board: H. Russell Bernard, Kathy Charmaz, D. Jean Clandinin, Juliet Corbin, Carmen de la Cuesta, John Engel, Sue E. Estroff, Jane Gilgun, Jeffrey C. Johnson, Carl Mitcham, Katja Mruck, Judith Preissle, Jean J. Schensul, Sally Thorne, John van Maanen, Max van Manen

Qualitative Essentials is a book series providing a comprehensive but succinct overview of topics in qualitative inquiry. These books will fill an important niche in qualitative methods for students—and others new to the qualitative research—who require rapid but complete perspective on specific methods, strategies, and important topics. Written by leaders in qualitative inquiry, alone or in combination, these books will be an excellent resource for instructors and students from all disciplines. Proposals for the series should be sent to the series editor at explore@lcoastpress.com.

Titles in this series:

1. *Naturalistic Observation,* Michael V. Angrosino
2. *Essentials of Qualitative Inquiry,* Maria J. Mayan
3. *Essentials of Field Relationships,* Amy Kaler and Melanie A. Beres

Essentials of Field Relationships

Amy Kaler
Melanie A. Beres

Routledge
Taylor & Francis Group
LONDON AND NEW YORK

First published 2010 by Left Coast Press, Inc.

Published 2016 by Routledge
2 Park Square, Milton Park, Abingdon, Oxon OX14 4RN
711 Third Avenue, New York, NY 10017, USA

Routledge is an imprint of the Taylor & Francis Group, an informa business

Copyright © 2010 Taylor & Francis

All rights reserved. No part of this book may be reprinted or reproduced or utilised in any form or by any electronic, mechanical, or other means, now known or hereafter invented, including photocopying and recording, or in any information storage or retrieval system, without permission in writing from the publishers.

Notice:
Product or corporate names may be trademarks or registered trademarks, and are used only for identification and explanation without intent to infringe.

Library of Congress Cataloging-in-Publication Data

Kaler, Amy.
  Essentials of field relationships / Amy Kaler and Melanie A. Beres.
    p. cm. — (Qualitative essentials)
  ISBN 978-1-59874-331-9 (hardcover : alk. paper) — ISBN 978-1-59874-332-6 (pbk. : alk. paper)
  1. Ethnology — Fieldwork. 2. Sociology — Fieldwork. 3. Social sciences — Fieldwork. I. Beres, Melanie A. II. Title.
  GN346.K36 2010
  301.072'1–dc22
                         2010010038

ISBN 978-1-59874-332-6 paperback
ISBN 978-1-59874-331-9 hardcover

Contents

Preface **7**

Chapter 1: Introduction **9**

Chapter 2: Transitioning In and Out of the Field **15**

Chapter 3: Maintaining Relationships in the Field **31**

Chapter 4: Establishing and Negotiating a Researcher Identity **57**

Chapter 5: Gathering Data **73**

Chapter 6: Research Ethics **91**

Chapter 7: Concluding Thoughts **107**

Notes **113**

References **117**

Index **123**

About the Authors **127**

Preface

For most readers, this book won't be your first introduction to social research. Whether you're a graduate student, a research fellow, a staff researcher or a seasoned professional, you've probably already learned quite a bit about research from classes, workshops or texts. Often these sources focus on research methods and the tasks involved directly with the research process—that is, different ways to collect and analyze data. This book, by contrast, explores another equally important area of conducting research: the social connections that researchers develop over the course of their research with participants and other stakeholders. These connections are what make data collection possible from the time you get access to a community setting; through the gradual development of rapport and mutual respect (or not, as the case may be); to the post-research period, when you leave your fieldwork site on good terms or bad.

Sometimes, the complexities of social relationships will make you want to tear your hair out and retreat back to armchair theorizing; sometimes these relationships will mark the high point of your research career, and sometimes, both will happen at the same time. Each research experience is unique and there will inevitably be many surprises along the way. Through this text we hope to alert you to some of those potential surprises and encourage you to think through some of them so that you may be better equipped to deal with surprises as they arise in your work. This is not a text outlining the "how to's" of fieldwork, but we pull together the experiences and lessons from the field of experienced researchers so that you can learn from those of us who have been there and can then perhaps avoid making some of the same mistakes as us (and likely discover new ones). This text focuses on examples and the experiences of seasoned researchers. As such, we do not focus on methodological debates in this area. Throughout the text we provide endnotes that point the reader to other sources for a more detailed philosophical and methodological discussion of issues raised in this text.

We would like to thank all those who contributed to the creation of this book, particularly the researchers who allowed us to share their stories and learn from their experiences: jimi adams, Nicole Angotti, Melanie Beres, Kim Berman, Jillian Carman, Kim Yi Dionne, Paul Hubbard, Amy Kaler, Thomas Molony, Kim Ro, Guy Thompson, Rebecca Thornton, Jenny Trinatopoli, Emilie Venables, Susan Watkins, Hui Niu Wilcox, and Anika Wilson. These people responded to our email and phone requests for "lessons from the field," and their stories, with identifying details removed, are scattered through this book. (The "lessons from the field" which are drawn from previously published sources are acknowledged as such.) We'd also like to thank Janice Morse and Mitch Allen for supporting us through the editing process and for their patience as we worked through the book.

Chapter 1

Introduction

In order to explore the development of field relationships it is first necessary to define what we mean when we mention "fieldwork." The field has been described in many ways in different disciplines, across various research eras and to collect a multitude of types of data.[1] So, what is fieldwork?[2]

It might be easier to say what fieldwork is not. Fieldwork is not using data that someone else has collected, whether a census, a sample survey, or a collection of interviews. It is not sorting through an archive to unearth recorded information about life in times past or present. It is not setting up experimental conditions and then setting the experiment in motion. It is usually not done from the comfort of one's office, building up pen-and-paper (or keyboard) models of the social world. To us, fieldwork is the messy but exciting process of interacting directly with people to learn something about the way they live. When you are doing fieldwork, your data are the lived experiences of the people whom you want to know about. You can collect (or create) these data in many different ways—through classic ethnography, in which the researcher tries to become an "insider" to a setting; through action-research, in which research and transformative social change go hand in hand; through interviews and focus groups, in which the researchers ask directly about questions of interest; or through participant observation, in which the researcher is both an onlooker and an actor in the social processes s/he wants to learn about. Many research projects combine elements of several of these strategies, as well as many others. We do not presume to advocate one form of fieldwork over others; instead we focus on the challenges, both expected and not, which arise whenever, and however, you're "in the field."

The Geographic Field

We take a decidedly broad view of the "field," so that this book is relevant for those venturing to far off lands and for those researching in their own "backyard."[3] Social science researchers have come a long way from the days when anthropologists would travel for months (or years) at a time to a distant land to document the lives of "unknown" peoples. Of course this view of the field is still relevant today, and many researchers (not limited just to anthropologists) travel varying distances in a quest to answer their research questions. Other disciplines, such as sociology, have a longer tradition of trying to understand the social world nearer to hand. With the growth in interdisciplinarity over the last few decades, researchers have developed parallel approaches to researching local and distant environments. For the purposes of this text we intentionally include research projects that may be located geographically at a distance from the researchers' location, or in the same neighborhood. In addition, since research is increasingly taking place across multiple field sites (within one study) and in virtual sites, we also address these issues.

These latter two types of "fieldwork" (multi-sited and virtual) are becoming increasingly more common. Multi-sited research takes place in a variety of either geographical and/or organizational locales.[4] For example Kurutani (2004) conducted research with Japanese expatriates living in the United States. Her research took her to a number of different cities throughout the U.S. John Telfer (2004) also conducted multi-sited field work, but his work was spread out over a number of different organizations related to adoption, including groups for adoptive parents and other groups for adults who were adopted as children.

The World Wide Web has opened up many opportunities for fieldwork, and research in this area can bring with it many of the same things as research in the "real" world.[5] Depending on the type of research, access may have to be negotiated, relationships to those in the field have to be established and data collected. This type of research could include analysis of blogs or discussion board posts on particular topics, to ethnographies of particular online communities or virtual worlds.

The Social Field

In addition to the possibility of dealing with geographical distance when conducting research, researchers must also be prepared for, and adapt to, varying levels of social distance between themselves and their research participants. The concept of "culture" has broadened beyond the notion of "culture" as something bounded by ethnicity or geography,[6] to include the idea that groups of people within a particular environment in particular settings might also have their own culture, which they share with distant others. The rapidly globalizing "hip hop" culture is one such example, for example, or we can also think of cliques or friendship networks in workplaces as having their own culture.

When talking of culture and social distance, scholars have historically used the term "insider" to describe a researcher familiar with, and part of, the social group he or she is researching, while "outsider" is used to describe someone working in a novel social setting.[7] Of course, the division between insider and outsider is a tenuous one at best, and one that is not necessarily helpful to define a researcher's position within the field. We are always at least partially an insider and partially an outsider in every project. The task then is not how to become an insider to connect with participants, or how to remain an outsider to allow for "objective" field work. It is about recognizing the connections we can make with those participating in our research in addition to those places and times when we come from different "places," and to think about how this impacts the research process, our relationships with the participants, and the outcome of the research project.

It is easy to think about instances where a researcher travels far from home to conduct ethnographic research, but those staying close to home have many of the same issues to think about regarding their fieldwork. They have to develop contacts, build relationships, develop an understanding of the environment they are researching, find participants, and leave the field site. Even if they are already intimately familiar with the field site, entering it as a researcher inevitably brings some of the same issues as any other research.

This Book

In the next chapter we open with issues involved with entering and leaving the field. Topics include how to choose a field location, how you can prepare before you start your research, things to think about while you are conducting your research, and how to be mindful of your participants as you think about ending your time in the field and going "home."

In chapter 3 we discuss how to maintain various relationships in the field. We start with discussing issues related to the "outsider" and "insider,"[8] then question the boundaries between those two categories and look at how we are most often simultaneously both insiders and outsiders. We also take a look at various hierarchical relations sometimes necessary for fieldwork including how to negotiate relationships with research assistants and supervisors. We encourage novice researchers to think carefully about whom they are accountable to and how they can best manage those relationships. Finally, we provide "food for thought" about some potentially tricky personal situations that may arise during fieldwork including personal (and maybe sexual) relationships that might develop or requests for funds and other support from participants.

Chapter 4 focuses on issues related to researcher identity. We revisit the issue of "insiderness" and "outsiderness" and how personal identity characteristics can contribute to and influence the research process. The focus is on providing suggestions to sensitize researchers to issues of identity, rather than outlining how particular identity characteristics may come into play. We pay particular attention to the sometimes unexpected issues around identity that can arise: we question the assumption that sameness (or sharing characteristics) leads to "insiderness" or that difference leads to "outsiderness," and we suggest that the ways that a researcher's identity is perceived is just as (if not more) important as the way that a researcher defines his or her own identity. We also discuss ways to balance multiple forms of identity during a research project and what to expect when these identities collide with one another (because they often do).

Chapter 5 is dedicated to data collection and outlines ways to facilitate the processes of collection during the fieldwork. Rather than focusing on methodology, we explore the social and practical requirements of collection. These include basics around dealing with equipment and technology and expand to how to deal with the unexpected during fieldwork. Unexpected events could mean changing the focus of the research project, or changing the nature and/or location of the fieldwork.

In the final substantive chapter we discuss research ethics. We talk briefly about institutional ethical review boards, but the major focus is on ethical behavior in the field. We outline two approaches to ethical conduct (minimalist and maximalist ethics) and discuss what these mean and the implications of using these different approaches to ethics.

The two authors of this book have spent most of their careers in various "fields," as PhD students, postdocs, junior and tenured faculty members, and contract researchers. We have worked independently and as members of bigger teams; we have been principal investigators, collaborators, and assistants. We haven't done it all, but we have collectively done enough to have built up some hard-earned knowledge about what to do (and more important, what not to do) to maximize the chances of research success. Throughout this book, we draw on this knowledge, and we refer to specific incidents in our own experiences. As mentioned earlier, we also bring in specific stories from other researchers who undertook fieldwork and lived to tell about it, in the form of boxed "lessons from the field." Some of these have been previously published; others were generously provided to us by colleagues and friends. In the latter case, identifying information has been omitted.

Chapter 2

Transitioning In and Out of the Field

So, you've decided on a research topic (finally!), have your data collection tools ready and are prepped for getting in and "doing" your research. It's time to move from planning research to actually doing it, but how do you start? Whom do you talk to? What steps can you take to ensure a relatively smooth data collection process? Data collection can be one of the most tenuous parts of the research process; it is a time when your research goals hinge on the generosity of others.

As social science researchers we need people to facilitate and participate in our research in order for it to be successful. This could mean granting access to a set of archives, or it could mean sharing a bit about themselves by volunteering to fill out a survey, to be interviewed or to take pictures and videos documenting their everyday lives. That is the "social" part of social science research. So how we approach people, whom we approach and what access we can get can literally make or break our project, and could mean the difference between a relatively straightforward project and one that is drawn out and difficult. Of course, because we rely on others, there is a lot that can be beyond our control, but let us take a look at some things we can do.

At this point we would like to take some time to outline some thoughts and suggestions about transitioning in and out of the field.⁹ This process should really begin when you are in the thinking and planning stages of your project and continues until after you've finished your data collection.

Planning the Research

The first step is to find the "field." As discussed in chapter 1, the field can be quite broadly defined and could mean that you stay comfortably in your own home, or that you go to a distant land far from home, or anything in between. Your field could be a social or geographical space which is completely novel to you, or it could be somewhere you already "speak the language," literally and figuratively. The process of entering the field really begins as you think about your topic of interest, your research question and the methods you choose to use. Thinking about gaining access to the field can play a large part of the design of the final project—a research project that is unique, theoretically engaging, and enormously useful can only go so far if it is not also practical and viable. In the planning stages here are some things to consider:

1. Where will you get the best data?

This question might sound obvious, but sometimes where we get the best data may not be the first place we think to look. It is important to think through your research question carefully and think about who can give you the answers to your questions. If using quantitative methods, then researchers need to be concerned with having enough people who fit their participant pool, so you may want to go where there is a high concentration of the phenomenon you are interested in. In some cases the virtual space of the Internet may be the easiest "place" to find people. Qualitative researchers are not only looking for a critical mass of people with relevant histories or experiences, but also for people who are willing to explore the issues with the researcher and are willing to talk. Your choice of field thus needs to suit your method as well as your topic or research question.

For example, Melanie wanted to study casual sex among young adults. Some quantitative researchers had already successfully surveyed young adults about their casual sex experiences while on spring break (see Maticka-Tyndale et al. 2003). However, considering the short duration of the time away, the commitment it takes to conduct an interview and the reported level of alcohol consumed, it may not be the most ideal place for in depth conversations about these experiences with a researcher. Melanie found that the best data (from the most reflective and engaged participants) were from those who had time to reflect back on their casual sex experiences (who were a little older) rather than those who were just beginning to experiment with casual sex. So, in this case the best data would not come from young people on break for a week, but from those who have had a bit of time to reflect on their experiences.

2. Where is the easiest place to get data?

The place to get the best data may not be the same as the easiest place to get data. If you are interested in studying Tibetan monks, the best place to go may be Tibet, but that is not likely the easiest place to access data (depending on the researcher's location), and it may be beneficial to try and find an alternative. As Telfer discovered there may also be social relationships that can facilitate or hinder data collection.

Lesson from the field:

Indeed, from the outset of fieldwork, my status as an intercountry adoptive parent proved to be something of a paradox. I soon became used to being introduced in some groups as "Jon Telfer, he's doing research on adoption and he wants to come to all our support group meetings and stuff—it's okay, though, he has adopted daughters, so he knows about adoption." In such situations, my status as having personal experience with adoption was represented as a distinct advantage. In other groups, however, this same status was a distinct disadvantage. Winning the trust of a particular group organized around adult adoptees was far from straightforward, for example. Some eight to ten weeks into fieldwork, I learned of this group through a social worker in the government department administering the release or withholding of information about adoptees and birth relatives. (Telfer 2004, 75-76)

One possibility that should not be overlooked is to tap personal contacts and networks with whom you already have connections. If you are acquainted with potential stakeholders—people who might have an interest in the outcome of the research, even if they don't participate in it directly themselves—these people may be able to point you in the right direction. You may also want to contact other people who have conducted research with similar populations and ask about the challenges and successes they had.

Most researchers are happy to field inquiries from people who are interested in the same questions that they are, and you shouldn't be shy about sending out emails or letters of inquiry, even if you know the other researchers only from their names on published articles. They may even be able to introduce you to some key people. When Melanie was deciding where she would go to collect data she sent letters to organizations in two different communities. There was no response at all from one community, and she got a chilly response during follow-up phone calls. In the other community the organization was extremely helpful and ended up playing a key role in data collection.

Despite the importance of personal contacts and relationships, choosing a field location is not only about whom you know, or whom you can meet, but also about other field conditions that affect data collection. It is helpful to consider other issues like travel, weather (the monsoon season, for instance, may not be the best time for data collection), and religious or cultural holidays that may impact schedules and availabilities. If your field is a workplace, for instance, variations in workflow may affect whether potential participants are willing or available to spend time with you. You may not want to schedule intensive interviewing at The Disney Store in the last two weeks of December, for instance.

Language is another issue to consider when choosing your field. If you do not speak the language spoken by your population of interest, what will you do? Will you do your interviews with an interpreter? If so, how will you find that person and ensure that he or she understands what you want from translation? Or will you immerse yourself in the culture in order to learn the language? If so, can you get up to an adequate fluency by the time fieldwork starts? Acquiring linguistic competence almost always takes longer than people expect, and if you plan to transcribe interviews or questions in a foreign language, you should expect to spend much longer in transcription.

Even if you are not going far from home and you are researching a group that shares your language, it's important to think more about language as a marker of "in-group" status. Is there a technical language that you should become familiar with? For instance, many professions have both official and unofficial jargon used to communicate with one another, and different social groups may have different slang or euphemisms for sensitive topics. Of course there are also benefits to not understanding some of the jargon and having your participants explain it to you. If you are really familiar with the participants' jargon (especially if it is also part of your personal language), you run the risk of simply assuming a shared meaning and understanding with your participants, without testing that assumption. By being somewhat naïve, you then have to ask participants to define what they mean, and you may get richer data this way.

As with all methodological decisions, of course, there is no right way or wrong way; each decision or attribute will have its benefits and its drawbacks. A researcher who is intimately familiar with the language of her or his participants might still ask for clarification and assume a naïve position to get different and deeper answers to a question.

The Boundaries of the Field: Time and Space

Where exactly is the field? There's a big difference between being able to point to a location on a map and having a clear idea of where the boundaries of your field are.[10] Most social science researchers want to study processes and relationships, not just collect descriptive information about events. Often, these processes and events lead us away from what we initially envisioned as the field and into other social locations. For instance, in Rachel Chapman's investigation of determinants of maternal health in Mozambique, her efforts to understand why pregnant women often avoided the government antenatal clinics led her away from the village she initially intended as her field site, into local government offices and even further afield (Chapman 2004). In theory, Chapman's investigations could have taken her to New York, to the headquarters of the World Bank or the International Monetary Fund, in order to get to the roots of the processes by which these Mozambican women were deprived of high-quality care.

Like Chapman, you too may be studying a process which transcends the time-and-space boundaries of the place you think of as your field, and like her you will need to decide how far you want to follow these processes. You may need to seek a balance between detailed knowledge of a particular field and detailed knowledge of a process or set of processes. How to strike this balance for analytical purposes will depend on the intellectual framework you want to create for your data, and we can't give you a prescription for how to reach that balance.

The boundaries of your field have a time as well as space dimension—when will you be officially "in the field," and when will you be out of researcher mode? If you're going somewhere far away, the dates on your air ticket will force you into a specific time frame. However, if your field overlaps with your home base, it may be more difficult to determine when you've finally left the field. You can't live in the data collection phase forever, and so if your field and your home are the same, you'll need to determine when to stop gathering data. The decision to stop collection at a certain point is inevitably arbitrary, and it's almost guaranteed that as soon as you decide your data collection is over, some particularly fascinating opportunity or event will present itself.

Some researchers limit the time spent in the field by a set of activities to be carried out—a certain number of interviews, a certain number of focus groups or hours of observation. If you use this numerical approach, it's a good idea to always plan on doing more interviews, focus groups, observations, etc. than you think you will actually need. For instance, in a recent project Amy determined that she would need a sample of 25 interviews to be reasonably sure she had adequate coverage of the population in question. However, she assumed that at least some of the interviews would turn out to be unintelligible, too short, or otherwise difficult to analyze, and so she planned to carry out 30 instead. By creating a "cushion" of 10%-25% more data than you expect to need, you can avoid last-minute panics when it's time to go.

Some other researchers use less quantitative measures, like "saturation," to determine when it's time to move on from data collection. (Saturation refers to the practice of collecting data until you reach a point of rapidly diminishing returns, when each additional interview, for instance, adds nothing or very little to the knowledge you have already acquired about the phenomenon.[11]) Just as with numerical counts of research activities, if you're relying on measures like "saturation", it's always wise to go beyond what you think is the minimum required amount of data collection. If you believe you've reached saturation in your data collection, it's worth taking a second look and asking yourself if you're truly "saturated" or if you're just getting a little bored and therefore less curious about what your data hold.

Multiple Fields

With multi-sited research, you may have to "enter" the field on multiple occasions and at different times.[12] Getting into the field may also be quite different in each setting. Doing research on your locations ahead of time may help. This could mean developing a sense of the organizational culture of the various organizations you are working with. For example, while conducting ethnography of adoption, David Telfer had to juggle different issues in various types of sites. Some organizations assumed an over-familiarity with David because of his status as an adoptive parent, while others were suspicious and interrogated him about his views before he was allowed to enter (Telfer 2004). Of course some multi-sited research takes place in various locations around the globe, and each city would then demand its own process of familiarization, including the logistics of getting around, accommodation, weather, and food as well as more subtle aspects of the culture of the place that may make it easier or more difficult to "get in."

Virtual Communities

Researching through the Internet and other "virtual" spaces is becoming more and more common. It can be a great way to locate underrepresented groups, or communities of people interested in an unusual hobby such as egg shell carving or for research dealing with personal and sensitive issues.[13] There are online communities for a huge number of things, and these can definitely be a worthwhile resource. Depending on the type of community you wish to research, entry into it may be relatively easy, or quite complex. For groups in the public domain it may be as easy as signing up, or even just browsing entries, but for more personal groups (like sexual abuse survivor support groups) you may have to go through a process similar to that for "actual" groups. Of course, considering that the community is virtual, the possibility of covert research is potentially endless (there are many ethical implications of this that we mention in chapter 6, but that are not discussed in depth in this volume).

Perhaps the biggest decision related to gaining entry when researching a virtual community is whether to do covert research or not. By doing covert research entering is easy as the researcher can either pose as part of the community or become a "voyeur" whose presence may or may not be seen by those participating in the group. If the researcher becomes visible as a researcher, than many of the same issues apply to researching in virtual communities in terms of getting permissions to enter and building rapport.

Into the Field

You are now ready to go, you've planned your research project, received the necessary ethical approvals, made your travel arrangements (whether it's a trans-continental flight or putting on your walking shoes) and have all your data collection tools printed and ready to go (don't forget extra batteries for your recorders!). At this point you have (ideally) established a couple of contacts in the field or have some ideas of how to do so. It may be helpful to take some time to acclimatize to the field and get a sense of how things work and how you will fit into the setting. If you are doing research at home in your current geographical location, you will have already accomplished this work. You have information on where particular groups spend time, which coffee shops are the trendiest, which paths are the most popular. You probably have an understanding of what is considered acceptable behavior—where it is okay to put up posters, or how to approach strangers. It may sound really simple, but Melanie spent a good amount of time on one project putting up posters in rather useless places, and having many taken down because she was not familiar with the campus and how things worked and the regulations around such things. You also understand the local language, slang and euphemisms which can help to make connections with people and get participants. You probably have a few contacts already so it would be helpful to start with them.

Lesson from the field:

New York was the hardest place to get my fieldwork going. I had no local lead to begin with, and when I arrived in my field site and began to call every expatriate Japanese organization I could think of, I found them to be extremely challenging to work with. Many of them had an official front person—a public relations manager, for example— whose job it is to screen and guard against unwanted outsiders penetrating their organization. I was often politely but decisively brushed off, referred to other organizations, denied information, and even discouraged from doing my research all together. It was partly the "big city" mentality that got in my way, but it also reminded me of living in Japan, where personal introduction is everything.

The only organization that was open to my research was... a grass-roots group of Japanese Americans in and around New York that also included some expatriate members. Although I met a few Japanese corporate wives through [this organization], I was still unable to enter this exclusive expatriate Japanese community....

In the end the answer was back home. Realizing that the great majority of expatriate Japanese in New York came

> *from Tokyo headquarters of the respective companies, I decided that I needed to work my way in from the other side of the Pacific Ocean. My only "business" contact in Tokyo was, unfortunately, my father.... A few days after talking with my father about finding contacts in the New York area, he faxed me a list of five individuals... who were "more than happy" to help me with my research "in any way possible." Two of them called me before I even had the chance to call them. (Kurotani 2004, 206-20)*

Throughout the research process it is important to remember that (in most cases) the people you interact with (including participants and people who grant access to their organizations or localities) will not benefit in any direct way from your research. Even in cases where you are attempting to create change for them, they may not see this as a benefit of their participation. Therefore, it is important to always treat these relationships with respect, and to try and find ways to give back to the community. What you do and how you do it may depend on how much energy and time you request from your participants or organizations that helped you through it. Melanie volunteered with one organization that was instrumental in her gaining access to the community and also let her use their (already tight) office space for interviews. In return, she not only shared her research results with them, but also helped in the planning of community events and staffed the office when no one else was around to field calls and handle drop-ins.

Depending on your particular field it may be appropriate to volunteer your services in ways that will help the local community, or if working with an underprivileged group (in the developing world for example), monetary or other types of subsistence donations may be appropriate. It might be helpful to check out what other researchers have done. One colleague of ours began a women's collective and sells baskets made by women in the local community in Uganda to her friends, family and acquaintances back home in Canada with all the money going back to the women in Uganda.

Some groups who have been heavily researched (often with less than ideal consequences) may be difficult to enter and may have established expectations around what is required of researchers in order to gain entry. For example, researchers interested in working with Aboriginal communities in Canada must demonstrate that they are committed to helping the community and must become invested in the community. As such, it is expected that members of the Aboriginal community have input into the research process including the research questions. Considering colonial legacies that have misrepresented and damaged communities of people, it is not surprising that Aboriginal communities are now demanding more of researchers. In Canada, the major funding institutions have a separate section in their ethics guidelines for researchers interested in studying within Aboriginal communities (see chapter 6). For researchers interested in working with such communities they have to be in a position to invest within such a community. It may not be possible for a graduate student to conduct a short project within such a community, unless he or she is a part of that community, or is willing to continue to be a part of it after the research is complete. Transitioning into a research setting is a continuous process of negotiation. If someone thinks you are not treating the community with respect, your access could be revoked either literally, in terms of physical access, or figuratively in the way that people may begin to react and respond to you differently. Of course, it may be nothing that you have done, but rather the nature of your research that may make people uncomfortable, and they may attempt to alter your progress.

This became abundantly clear for a student of Melanie's who was trying to do a short research project with an organization that provides services to Aboriginal populations. Initially the organization seemed supportive, but upon learning that the student was not Aboriginal (she was a Native Studies student), her access to the organization was effectively cut off (although she was not told this directly). Her project became a reflexive project about her experience in light of what she was learning in her Native Studies courses. There are similar guidelines and research practices expected for researchers interested in other indigenous groups around the world

When dealing with sensitive topics and potentially disenfranchised groups it is important to research ahead of time the necessary protocols for conducting the research within these groups. It could save being turned away from your research site of choice and having to dramatically change your research project.

There is an important difference between formal entry into a setting, and the acceptance by participants who will then enable your research. Keep in mind the relationship between the people who granted you access and the people with whom you are interested in researching. If the relationship between these two groups is one of unequal power, then participants' perception of you will be at least partially determined by their impression of your relationship with those who authorized your access. Sometimes maintaining these relationships may involve some tensions and some masterfully diplomatic negotiation skills.

Lesson from the field:

My acceptance among the inmates has passed through several phases. When I first arrived, I was a welcome novelty for inmates and administrators alike—a stranger to show off to. Everyone wanted to be around me, to touch me, and to tell me their story. The boys ... approached me with the hopes of gaining a ... valuable gift, and thereby increasing their own status within the institution. This lasted three days. For the next two weeks of my research, I was given an office in a room shrouded in ill augury, where the then-administration decided I was to call individual inmates in for interviews. This situation cast me in a role similar to that played by the psychologists and social workers.... During this phase, I was generally considered an ally of the administration... which meant that the adults regarded me as an equal worthy of respect and the boys kept their distance... thankfully this uncomfortable stage of research was short-lived. The next phase of my research began after I returned from an unplanned, extended hiatus. I came back to the institution with a reinvigorated resolve to learn about the lives of the institution's inmates. I had gotten a reputation among them for integrity and I possessed a mark that earned me status among—and a measure of solidarity with—them: a scar from a nearly-fatal knife wound....[W]hen I resumed my daily visits to the institution, my place had been... (re)defined.... I was told that I was to stay inside the prison yard with the inmates, and out of the administrative building.

Ironically, nine months into my research at the institution, the administration suddenly decided to block my access to the yard..., claiming that it was a measure taken for my own protection.... When my permission to enter the [correctional institution] was suspended by the administration, I went over their heads and obtained judicial authorization to continue my work. In order to soften the blow to the authority of the institution's administrators that consent for my research would constitute, the judge allowed the administrators to impose "necessary" security measures to protect me and the inmates during my research, without interfering with the research itself. The measure that the administration implemented was that of the "intimate search." (Drybread 2006, 40-42)

Leaving the Field

Leaving the field may be easy and straightforward, but it can also be a sensitive process. For researchers working at home there may not really be a need to "leave" the field because it might be a site where you spend time on a regular basis. Of course, now that you've conducted research your relationship to the site and the people who make it up has changed, even though the change may be slight.

For some leaving the field might be easy and straightforward, and involve nothing more than getting on a plane or getting in your car. This was the case for Kristin Lozanski who conducted research with backpackers in India (Lozanski and Beres 2007). To do the research she went backpacking around India by herself. Because of the loose social networks, and because backpacking is a transient activity, she was constantly meeting and saying good-bye to participants throughout her fieldwork. Leaving India was no different than leaving any of the individual cities along her travels. Of course, even though she left she did maintain contact with many of her participants through email, and so the relationships she built did not end with the end of her fieldwork.

For researchers with more stationary research fields, leaving the field may involve saying good-bye to new friends and may not be so easy. When Melanie was getting ready to leave the field she slowed her participation in one of the activities of the young adults in the community—that of going to bars in the evening. One of her participants was quite concerned and asked her if she was sick because she missed a night at the bar. This was a good reminder to Melanie that even though she was upfront with people about why she was in town, some people saw her primarily as a friend.

Getting ready to leave the field is also a time to make sure that your data are organized and that you have all you need to get your research project to the next level. Sending copies of your data home (so they do not get lost with your luggage) may be something to consider. It might also involve details like canceling your local cellular telephone or other organizational tasks.

One of the most important leaving tasks is to acknowledge the contributions that people in the field have made to your project, and to lay the groundwork for future cordial relations (or at the very least, to leave on a high note!). Some researchers organize formal leave-taking events, during which they may present an overview of their research or otherwise feed back some of their work to the community. One colleague organized a photo exhibit at a community center, using pictures she and her research participants took while documenting economic transformations in the community. In some cultural contexts, it may be appropriate to provide a farewell meal, or to give speeches formally thanking people. In addition to public leave-taking, you should also consider more private acknowledgments to particular people. For instance, you can provide your research assistants with written recommendations they could use if they apply for similar jobs. Finally, there's no such thing as too many thank-you notes!

Even once you have physically left the research setting, you have in a way brought a part of the setting with you in the form of your data. You also have a whole new set of relationships that do not just end when you walk out the door or step on a plane.

Chapter 3

Maintaining Relationships in the Field

Most people contemplating fieldwork are preoccupied with the tasks at hand—figuring out what information you need, figuring out how to get it, and then figuring out what to do with it once you've gotten it. However, the world of fieldwork is much more complex than that simple task-centered environment you may imagine. By undertaking fieldwork, you are entering a universe of "others": people and groups whom you must negotiate with in order to get your work done. Depending on where your field is located, these others may be people you have known all your life with whom you must now forge new relationships centered on research; or people whose existence you may not even have been aware of when you were contemplating your project, pre-fieldwork, in blissful ignorance. In this chapter, we take on some of the issues involved in creating and sustaining relationships with these "others."

When You're an Outsider[14]

This is the situation that most people imagine when they think of fieldwork—the lone researcher coming into a community where s/he is a stranger, and slowly becoming a part of that community, if only for a short time. This sort of outsider fieldwork has advantages, but also presents challenges in terms of building and maintaining relationships with the people around you.

No one ever really starts with a blank slate when coming to do fieldwork in a community. While you as a person may be an unknown commodity, the community itself will have had experiences with other outsiders (unless you work in Antarctica), and the relations you are able to maintain with community members will be conditioned at least in part by their experiences or ideas about other visitors. Even before you arrive in your site, you should try to find out what the "outsider history" of your community is. Has the community recently hosted other researchers, missionaries, tourists, traveling medical or educational personnel? If so, did these people contribute much to the community? Or did any problems or conflicts arise? For example, Melanie's fieldwork in a small town was going well until the media began contacting her for interviews. One organization was strongly opposed to her talking with reporters. It turned out that a previous researcher painted the community in a negative light in a television show that was broadcast nationally. Having been burned by researchers once before, this particular organization was operating from a position of (justified) distrust when it came to hosting researchers.

In some parts of the world, communities may have had an overload of researchers, and people may be suffering from "research fatigue," not wanting to answer one more survey question or gather together for one more focus group. In this case, you may find that community expectations of research, and particularly of the material benefits to them of research, have preceded you. Potential participants may expect you to pay them, or get involved in community projects, or provide employment because former researchers did so.

Similarly, you may find yourself in the position of shaping the expectations which will meet future researchers, by your conduct and by your research design. In particular, if you offer incentives or pay people for participating, the same incentives and payments may be expected from the next research project to come down the road. This can cause tension between relatively wealthy researchers (such as those working for major foundations or organizations) who can afford to distribute money and goods and relatively "poor" researchers, such as graduate students, who don't have that same sort of budgetary leeway, even if they would like to be able to offer more remuneration to people who participate in their projects.

Lesson from the field:

Our site was "over-researched." Because it was relatively close to the city, many American researchers had passed through asking more or less the same kinds of questions as us. When we went to someone's home to interview them, we took along a bag of sugar as a gift, but we often got complaints that one bag of sugar wasn't enough, and other research teams had given them two, or had given them something better.

Even if your community hasn't been over-researched, your differences from community members will mark you in ways which may be outside your control. If you have the money and the leisure (or apparent leisure) to travel long distances just to ask questions, and very few people in the community could dream of such largesse, you may be regarded with envy, resentment or sycophancy by the people around you. You may also be seen as a bit peculiar if your research questions do not strike those around you as particularly interesting and relevant to their own lives.

The concept of academic research is not universal, and you should come up with ways to describe what you are doing which will make sense within the worldview of your participants. For instance, one colleague was doing oral history work in a place where the local language did not have a word for "research." With the help of his research assistant, he came up with a phrase to explain why he was traveling around asking people questions about their long-gone youth, which translates literally as "digging up knowledge." In another case, Amy explained her complicated research question, which involved such high-flown abstractions as discourse, power, resistance and agency as "learning about the health of mothers and babies." Being able to explain her project in these terms set people at ease, and made them less suspicious of the outsider from the university.

Local stereotypes, positive and negative, about people who share your gender, skin color or place of origin can also come into play. For these reasons, it's good to cultivate one or two trusted associates in your field site whom you can ask about stereotypes and whether or not your behavior is conforming to them. For instance, clothing which is considered perfectly acceptable in some North American contexts, such as tank tops or shorts, may be seen as provocative in other settings, making the wearer vulnerable to the stereotype of the sexually loose and available foreigner. If you have a friend or an associate whom you can trust to be straightforward with you about whether you're accidentally fulfilling negative preconceptions about people of your kind, you can head off some trouble before it starts. The less you conform to group stereotypes, the more likely you are to be seen as an individual.

However, the individual that you are in fieldwork situations may not be the same individual that you are at home or in other social settings. Many researchers develop (consciously or not) a "field personality"—a version of themselves in which traits which are conducive to good fieldwork, such as enthusiasm, patience and a sense of humor, are maximized. In developing a fieldwork personality, you are not necessarily being a hypocrite by putting together a version of yourself which is slightly different than the version which you put together for an outing with friends or a family get-together, or even other professional contexts. Sociologists call this "deep acting"—incorporating the emotions, perspectives and behaviors which enable you to function in a setting with minimal emotional stress and disappointment.

Twenty-first century North American society typically puts a premium on "being yourself" and asserting your unique personality, but in the field, such persistent self-assertion can turn into rigidity. Being able to take up a fieldwork personality when appropriate is a skill which can be just as important as being competent in your chosen methodology.

Whatever version of yourself you bring to fieldwork, one of the keys to success as an outsider is to speak less than you hear. Particularly in the early stages of your fieldwork, keeping relatively quiet and observing what's going on around you (even if you find some of what's going on troubling) will serve you better than offering up opinions and expressing them freely before you really understand what is going on. This doesn't mean you should retreat into moral relativism and make no (silent) judgments on things you find disturbing, but it does mean that if you decide to address these disturbing things later, you'll have a better chance of doing so in a locally appropriate way.

At the same time, don't shy away from asking questions. Most people in most places are happy to talk about their homes and communities, and will appreciate a show of genuine interest from a visitor. In your early days in the field, you should try to identify at least one person to whom you would feel comfortable asking questions about the way life is carried out, even questions that seem dumb or potentially awkward. Asking such questions should be done in private, not in a public space.

As an outsider without prior connections in your community, your primary, and possibly only, identity in the field will be "researcher." Of course, in your real life you are many things besides a diligent researcher, and you have many facets of your personality which can't be expressed if you're always locked into that one identity. For this reason, you should be careful to schedule down time for yourself, when you can put research aside and mentally escape for a little while. If you're doing a long stint away from home, having magazines and newspapers from home can provide this sort of escape; even if you're doing a short stint, Internet connections and DVDs or CDs can take you out of research mode. However, try not to let these things become too prominent in your life in the field. Don't let yourself become dependent on reminders of home—this will only make you miserable, and won't help the time pass any better.

Lesson from the field:

"The more connected I become with those I have left behind, the more alone I feel in Senegal," my fieldwork diary reads. On my pre-Internet Africa trips, I had very few reminders of 'home'. There were no daily emails, no text messages and definitely no Skype. I didn't miss things because, quite simply, I didn't remember them. Now, instead of waiting for airmail letters that may never come, and not hearing from my friends for six months, my Senegalese life is punctuated with daily reminders of England. The BBC website keeps me updated on the world outside, the short-wave radio on which I once depended for crackling snippets of international news lying dormant in my trunk. I form an unhealthy addiction to 'feel-good' stories from local English newspapers. The kind of articles I would never read 'back home' now appeal to me, and allow me to momentarily forget the dust and heat and hassle outside my door. The ease in which I can temporarily remove myself from Senegal makes me question the quality of my fieldwork and the extent to which I am integrating. I feel guilty for

retreating into my half-built house to watch a DVD instead of drinking my third round of attaya [sweetened green tea], wonder if I am harming my research by reminding myself of another world. I try to manage my multiple identities and responsibilities as much as I can, resisting the urge to become part of the ex-pat world I have always shunned, as the comfort it would offer feels like a step too far. I seek to balance the two places I call home, searching for a way to stay in touch with my English past whilst thriving in my Senegalese present.

When You're an Insider

For some researchers embarking on fieldwork, the field is terra incognita. They enter into the social space of the field as researchers, without prior commitments or relationships. For others, however, "the field" may also be their home, or their community of origin, or their workplace, or some other social space in which they have built up ties and connection over years. If you're in this latter group, you will have to navigate the field while carrying many expectations from the people around you. They know you as a relative, a neighbor, a co-worker, a member of a particular group, but you now reappear in a different guise, that of researcher, layered on top of (and often in conflict with) your other identities. For simplicity's sake, we will refer to all of these situations in which you are not an outsider as situations in which you are in your own community.

Reams and reams have been written about the benefits and challenges of doing research in your own community. We are not going to reiterate this extensive literature here, but will focus on some ways to head off or at least to minimize potential difficulties with being an "insider."

In these situations, it's important to be absolutely clear with yourself and with others as to what your research is all about, what information you will collect and what you will do with it, and when you are or aren't in "research mode." You also need to be clear what sorts of outcomes the people around you can (or can't) expect from your work, as a result of your prior membership in the community. For instance, you can't breach the confidentiality of your informants to satisfy the curiosity of your friends or relatives about who in the community is doing what. Similarly, you can't promise that benefits to your community will flow from your research, unless of course you're sure these benefits will materialize. However, you can promise to let your community know the outcomes of your research (through formal presentations, or through short articles in local media or newsletters). You should be sure that you don't give particular people or groups privileged access to your findings, but instead keep outcomes in the public domain, as far as possible.

You should also think through the possibilities for maintaining boundaries between yourself-as-researcher and yourself-as-community-member, particularly if you're undertaking qualitative forms of research such as ethnography or participant observation. Remaining constantly in research mode is exhausting, and potentially alienating to your friends and colleagues. Give yourself time to put your notebooks and surveys away; and think carefully about the ethical issues involved in transferring material from your real life (conversations you've taken part in, things that you notice when you're not officially in research mode) into your data collection. As a member of the community, you will have privileged access to understanding the social dynamics of your field site, but with that privileged access comes responsibility.

If, in the course of your research, you come up with material that is potentially embarrassing to your community, you may feel intense internal and external pressure to suppress or alter the information for the sake of community loyalty. In this situation, you may need to think about what the consequences for you as a member of the community will be if you do go ahead with potentially embarrassing research. Remember, though, that communities are made up of diverse and sometimes conflicting interest groups, and for every person who doesn't want you to find and air dirty laundry, there is undoubtedly another person who wants these uncomfortable truths to become known. If you're in this position, consider how you might analyze and present this information in a way which suggests constructive solutions to community problems, rather than a way which can be read simply as denunciation of bad practices. You may want to think about whether it is better for an insider (you) or an outsider (a colleague, or someone else) to handle this information.

Finally, be prepared for psychological awkwardness as you transition from one identity within your community (as a child, a friend, a worker, etc.) to another (as a researcher). You should also be prepared for the possibility that the transition back to your old identity, once the research is complete, may not be smooth. You'll be a very different sort of daughter, friend or co-worker as a result of having looked at your community through new eyes, the eyes of a researcher

Hierarchical Relationships

One basic sociological tenet is that all social settings are permeated with power—the power to make things happen, the power to influence others, the power to determine the course of future events. The allocation of power in some settings may strike you as inequitable, and you may want to subvert it or challenge it in some way. The ethics of creating change in a fieldwork situation are discussed elsewhere, and in general, it's difficult for a lone researcher to make substantial changes in his or her field. To carry out your research, then, you will most likely have to work within the power relations that you encounter.

Hierarchies are often difficult to figure out. As anyone who's ever worked in an organization knows, the people who are formally or officially in charge of things may or may not be the people who are actually able to get things done. And as anyone who has ever been in junior high knows, friendship ties and cliques may be as important as more formal considerations when it comes to how things get done. In your fieldwork, you will need to understand both the formal and the informal rules about how things get done, or don't get done.

If you are working in an economically marginalized part of the world, it's important to remember that global asymmetries of power interact with situational asymmetries of power. For instance, if you are a graduate student, although you may be at the bottom of the ladder in your home university, you may find that you have riches and resources far beyond those commanded by your colleagues and your superiors in the field. At the same time, these global asymmetries do not necessarily determine who is more powerful than whom in the immediate local context. You may be wealthy and powerful by local standards, but compared to people whose power resides in their age, their life experience or their practical knowledge, you may be in a very dependent position indeed. If you are entering a fieldwork situation where you don't have prior knowledge of how the hierarchies work, the best advice is to keep quiet, observe, and treat everyone, including yourself, with as much respect as possible.

Lesson from the field:

We arrived at the Health Center around 1:30pm. There were about 40 people of all ages with health passports in hand, sitting patiently on the cement benches facing the door to the office of the medical assistant. [My driver] said something to the patients in chiChewa. All I understand from the exchange was 'mzungu' [white person], which made me incredibly uncomfortable; the exchange suggested that being a mzungu was about to award me a front of the line pass to the medical assistant's office. When a patient exited the office, Suzgo indicated to me that it was OK to go in. I looked at the group of patients embarrassed, and politely said, "zikomo" [excuse me]. They clapped their hands together, almost in unison, granting me permission to enter ahead of them. I have no doubt that they have been waiting, and will continue to wait, a very long time to be seen.

We entered the office and the Medical Assistant introduced himself. ... I explained to him that I'm a graduate student from America interested in learning more about HIV testing in Malawi. I asked if it would be possible to schedule appointments to speak with the HIV counselors. He replied that I am "most welcome" and that I should return Monday afternoon to meet with them. He asked that I sign the guest book before I leave. In the car, I told [my driver] I was uncomfortable going back on Monday without having asked the HIV counselors themselves if they were able and willing to meet with me. He told me not to worry and that the Medical Assistant would tell them that a 'mzungu' would like to speak with them. I replied, "Is that what he'll say?" He said yes, and then explained to me that Malawians want to give Americans a good impression of Malawi because 'America is a donor country'. I explained to him that I, myself, am not a donor.

For many people just starting out in a research career, being "the boss" may be novel and uncomfortable . If you are a graduate student or a junior researcher, you may have had little experience of being in charge of a project, yet fieldwork situations may require you to take charge of other people's work and tell them what to do. Creating and maintaining a productive and respectful relationship with the people who work for you can be an unexpected challenge in the field.

The most common hierarchical fieldwork relationship is that between a researcher and his or her research assistants (RA). The scope of an assistant's duties can vary widely, from typing in your survey data to translating your words for the community to providing complex specialized skills in the service of your project. In cases where an RA is simply saving you time by doing things which you could have done yourself, such as data entry, filing or other clerical work, the relationship can be quite straightforward—you tell the RA what you want them to do, check that they're doing it, and compensate them as agreed (all the while treating them, of course, as you would want a good boss to treat you).

However, if your RA provides skills and resources which you don't have, so that you are effectively dependent on him or her, relations can become more complicated. This is particularly true if your RA mediates between you and the community in which you are working—for instance, as an interviewer, a translator or a spokesperson. In these cases, you may find that your project is being shaped to a significant degree by someone whose formal role is simply to help you with "your" project, and that while you are nominally in charge, you are not making the actual daily decisions about how the work should be carried out. In this situation, if your RA's vision of the project and your vision of the project differ, you may be in for a surprise.

Lesson from the field:

I must confess that the promise of fieldwork was one of the main factors in my decision to become an archaeologist. The thought of a conventional desk-job repelled me, while the anticipation of sunny days spent in healthy exercise and the pursuit of knowledge was an irresistible combination. Consequently I decided to conduct my own survey as part of my honours dissertation. With the brash naivety of a 21-year-old, I aimed at intensively surveying a supremely rugged and hence under-explored area of 50km², in a quest for stone age and rock art sites which I could use to conduct spatial analysis utilising the flashy GIS program I had just acquired. This experience cemented my desire to become an archaeologist and taught me many valuable things, not least to develop a better appreciation of any study area before venturing in blindly. I learnt that one should always take great care to inform everyone involved what we are doing and why it is necessary. This was brought home when I overheard a landowner asking one of my field assistants why we were walking around looking at the ground and under the large boulders common to the area. He replied, "I'm not sure, but he [pointing to me] thinks it will make him smarter." Needless to say an "orientation session" for all involved was immediately held, and ever since then, an initial briefing is an integral part of any survey I do.

The best way to avoid such surprises is to be sure that you and your RAs share a depth of understanding of the purpose of the research, and of the ways that your chosen methodology will enable you to carry out that purpose. Some researchers, especially those coming from a participatory action or emancipatory research orientation, see this as an opportunity to invite RAs to be "co-creators" of research; while other researchers from more mainstream orientations see this as an imperative to facilitate your RAs' understanding of a project which has already been conceptualized and thought out. Regardless of where you find yourself on the spectrum between these orientations, here are some tools which can help you ensure that you and your RAs are on the same page:

Lesson from the field:

No one in Rwanda was better than my researchers at advising me on how much our participants felt constrained by government surveillance and at alerting me to nuanced signs of trust or suspicion. After the first pretest in Rwanda, the team agreed during a roundtable discussion that answers were routinely superficial for one particular question: "Would you share a beer with a person from another group?" (a standard social scientific question of social distance). One researcher suggested a simple but crucial variation on the question: Would you share a beer with a person from the 'other group', if the bottle was not opened in your presence? This variation touched upon the deep cultural suspicion of poisoning, and participant responses took an interesting and dramatic turn after we changed the question. I would not have been brave enough to break out of this standardized question had it not been for the insistence of the researchers and their own familiarity with the limits of public discourse in that context. (Paluck 2007, 14)

1. Training and dialogue

Don't skimp on training time, and don't treat training time as a one-way transfer of information. It may be tempting to head straight into data collection, but time spent familiarizing yourself and your research assistants with the protocols, guidelines and research questions you intend to use will be time well spent. Training time should also not consist entirely of you telling other people what you want them to do—gather your RAs' impressions of the work that you are asking them to do, be open to their ideas about how your plans might be improved, and work towards building a sense of ownership of "our" project.

2. Role-plays

Role-plays are a great way to check whether you and your RAs are on the same page (as well as a great tension-reducer and source of laughter). You can role-play almost any form of data collection that involves interaction with other people—surveys, interviews, observations, etc. Role-playing other forms of research, like archival searching or mapping, may be more difficult, but with a bit of imagination and preparation, this can be possible, too. When you do role-plays, be sure to throw some curve balls and include situations which you may not have explicitly addressed during training, to see how your RAs handle them.

3. Back-translation

Technically, back-translation refers to the process of preparing a survey written in one language for implementation in a different language. The survey is translated from language A into language B by one person, and then translated from language B back to language A by a second person. If the two language A versions are compatible, then the language B version is presumed to be an accurate reflection of the original. However, back-translation as a concept can be applied far beyond surveys. After you have explained and demonstrated what you want your RAs to do, you can ask them to "back-translate" by explaining and demonstrating for someone else (or for you, is no one else is available). If that third party understands the research tasks in the same way that you do, you can be fairly sure that you and your RAs are on the same page. You can also learn whether you're actually enabling RAs to build skills and acquire new competences as a consequence of being involved in your research, or whether they're just doing things in a rote fashion.

4. Constant debriefing

Once your research is underway, debrief with the RAs as often as possible. You can institute a daily meeting at the end of the workday, or every other day, for going over what happened that day, what challenges were encountered and what went well. This need only take a few minutes, but can let you know if unexpected issues are cropping up, as well as gather suggestions for how to deal with them. Constant debriefing is especially important if you never accompany your RAs on their work.

Boss or Friend?

If you're working in a cultural setting you are not familiar with, you should be attentive to local expectations of what an employer (you) should do for his or her employees (your RAs). In some settings, you may be called on to play a more involved role in the lives of your RAs than you expect. For instance, you may be asked to lend money or goods, to advocate for your RAs in other settings outside the work, and to contribute to important events in their lives or the lives of their families, such as weddings or funerals. If you regard your RAs as friends as well as assistants or co-workers, these expectations of involvement may well challenge the boundaries between researcher and assistant. You should think through how important it is for you to maintain those boundaries, and what might be the consequences, positive or negative, if the boundaries are breached. This is quite a personal matter—some people are most comfortable with firm boundaries, relating to the people they work with on a purely professional basis, while others are more comfortable becoming more involved as friends.

Problems can arise, however, when "being friends" and "getting the work done" become mutually exclusive. This problem can be particularly acute for female researchers, who may have experienced years of gender conditioning to "be nice" and make people happy. However, all researchers need to be prepared for the possibility they may be perceived as "not nice" or "a bad friend" in the course of getting their work done. The power differentials between researcher and assistant never disappear, no matter how friendly you may be, and may reappear at uncomfortable moments.

Lesson from the field:

[A supervisor] and [a data entry team member] failed to show up for work today. I had gone to eat lunch in town to see if it might ease my stomach pains, and when I returned to the data room they had still not yet arrived to work. I tried calling both of them by phone, but no answer. I asked the other members of the data team and received only silence and shrugged shoulders in return. I managed to find [the supervisor] tonight in his room, far too drunk to get any work done. He told me he was sick and that he would take care of whatever work I needed tomorrow morning. The problem is I needed that work done today for people to have in-hand when they leave for the field tomorrow morning. I don't know if I should let this guy go since I need him for this last week. I just don't want the other staff to think this kind of behavior would be overlooked at the end of fieldwork. I need everyone to be working. I eventually decided to keep the supervisor on staff. I docked him a day's pay and made him aware of my concern for his personal situation. The other staff member that failed to show up for the day was dismissed. This split decision was a difficult one for me to make, and I still wonder if it was, in the end, a fair decision. I needed to demonstrate to the rest of the staff that I was equally good at using negative as well as positive incentives to get the staff to work hard, but I was not about to fire the one person I knew I needed to get through the remaining fieldwork. I am not certain how my decision was received by the staff.

People to Whom You Are Accountable

Most field researchers, at least at the beginning of their research career, find themselves with two sets of people to whom they must be accountable—the people who are supervising or interested in the outcomes of the research, often from afar (your advisers, funders or sponsors) and people with whom you work in the field, who expect and are entitled to some sort of benefit from the research. Often, these two groups do not share the same sense of what research should be, nor the same vision of what exactly you should be doing. For instance, the academic concerns with matters like validity, reliability or replicability, depending on your epistemological model, may seem arcane to non-academics who just want to know what you found out or how it can be of use to them. The need for practical, specific solutions to specific problems expressed by people in the communities you work with may not be of interest to your academic supervisors, who are more concerned with how your work can help to advance theory in an academic discipline. If your research is being funded by an organization with its own agenda and interests, your funders may have quite a different idea of what you should be doing than you or the people around you do. It's not unusual for researchers to feel that they are caught, that they can't be properly accountable to one party without failing in their responsibilities to another.

Lesson from the field:

[M]y university's committee for the protection of human subjects did not approve of my proposal to conduct research in the prisons, because of the strict government control over which prisoners were allowed to participate. [The organization I worked with] was not willing to drop this aspect of the research design, so I conducted research in the prisons for the NGO [Non-Governmental Organization] in a purely "consultative" role and was prevented from reporting on data from the prisons in an academic setting. (Paluck 2007, 11)

In order to avoid problems cropping up in these relationships of accountability, consider the following:

1. Make it crystal clear to everyone with a stake in your project what you will be doing, and what exactly they can expect from you over the course of the project and at the end of it. In business jargon, this is called specifying the deliverables. The same information can be delivered in various different ways, depending on whom you are reporting to: as a dissertation or an academic article; as a memorandum or a position paper; as an oral presentation or workshop, etc. You can craft different products from the same data and analysis, tailored to the needs and interests of funders, local community members, academic supervisors, and the like.

2. If you are accountable to people who are not accessible on a daily basis, be sure you stay in close contact. Constant (written) contact not only keeps everyone on the same page, but also provides you with a record of the development and execution of your project, which may be invaluable once you've left the field. Email makes this task much easier. You may want to set up a schedule for emails to supervisors or funders, sending them updates once a week. You may also want to email your data back to them (suitably anonymized) in order to ensure you have a backup should something happen to your original files. It is also helpful to send an email summarizing a verbal meeting in order to confirm you are all on the same page and for future reference if required.

Tricky Interpersonal Situations

In your fieldwork, you may encounter some, all or none of these:

1. *Money—lending and borrowing.* If you are in a fieldwork situation in which you are, or are perceived to be, wealthier than most people, you may be asked for loans or outright

gifts of money. Several challenges can arise in these situations: You may not have the money that everyone thinks you do, and so may not be able to give it. Alternately, you may be financially able to lend or give money, but don't want to do so, whether because you don't approve of the purpose for which the loan is being requested, or because you don't want to be seen as a human ATM machine.

There is nothing wrong with making loans or gifts out of compassion, friendship, or the desire to help. In addition, lending money can be a form of reciprocity—if the people in your local community have given generously of their time and knowledge, without any direct compensation, helping out with financial difficulties can be one way of reciprocating. However, you should consider each loan as a potential gift—in other words, never lend more than you can afford to lose, and don't count on getting your money back. If lending money encourages financial dependency, you are doing no one a favor (including those researchers who come after you, who may have to deal with expectations that you've created, that all researchers coming into the community have deep and open pockets). If you are approached for financial assistance, see if there's any non-monetary way you can help in resolving the problem that led to the request—by giving a lift rather than giving money for transport, for instance, or by helping someone fix their radio rather than handing over money for a new one.

Lesson from the field:

I was tremendously impressed with the field director of our project and how he handled a potentially sticky situation. Some staff at the local clinic approached him for money on a Friday afternoon, saying that the clinic refrigerator was out of propane, and they had vaccines for childhood immunization days which had to be kept refrigerated, so they needed to buy propane. Our field director said that he sympathized, but instead of giving money, he would carry the vaccines back to our research base and keep them in our refrigerator over the weekend, and then the clinic staff could collect them on Monday morning. The staff didn't take him up on the offer. I don't know if there really was a propane shortage, or if the request for money was just a way for some unscrupulous staff members to get money for the weekend, but by offering the use of the fridge, our field director provided both parties with a face-saving solution.

---

2. *Sex*. Particularly if you're a newcomer to your field site, you may be sized up for your sexual potential (and may be doing some sizing-up of your own). Such sizing-up can range from the flattering to the threatening. If you want to discourage sexual attention, the best strategy is to claim prior commitments (fictitious boyfriends/girlfriends or spouses can come in handy here, as can purported religious commitments to monogamy or celibacy), rather than outright refusal. However, not all sexual tensions may be unwanted.

The general rule for beginning a sexual relationship during fieldwork, especially with someone from the community in which you are working, is "don't." You will inevitably be seen as someone whose professionalism and possibly even integrity has been compromised once you are known to be sexually active, particularly (and unfairly) if you are a woman. For women (and to a lesser extent, for men) a good rule of thumb is to behave like the most sexually conservative members of your gender in the community, until you've had a chance to figure out how sexual expression affects one's respect and status accorded by others. In many communities, there is no such thing as a "secret" liaison, especially if you as an outsider are a subject of scrutiny and interest. In addition, given the power dynamics which often exist between researcher and researched, as discussed above, your sexual relationship will inevitably be complicated by nagging questions of equality. However, if the attraction is irresistible and mutual, try to wait until after the period of fieldwork is officially over. This waiting period is essential if your paramour is someone over whom you have nominal authority, such as a research assistant. For those doing fieldwork away from home, remember, too, that although you will be going back to your pre-and post-fieldwork life, the people you become sexually involved with will be remaining in their community, and their status may be affected by their relations with you.

Sex in the field, however, doesn't always take the form of mutual attraction. Fieldworkers, particularly but not exclusively women, can be subject to unwanted sexual overtures, especially if they are new to the community and not obviously attached to someone. You should employ the same strategies and cautions that you would at home, and perhaps even more so. Some fieldworkers invent imaginary (and very protective) fiancés or spouses to discourage advances, which is generally more effective than conjuring up an imaginary boyfriend or girlfriend. Others pay attention to the dress and behavior of the most sexually conservative members of the community in which they are doing their research, such as older, married, churchgoing women, and then model their own dress and deportment on them, rather than on members of the community who are closer to the researcher in gender and life stage. For women in particular, it's also helpful to cultivate friendships with other local women, so that your social contacts and supports are not limited to men.

3. *Invitations.* If your work is going well and you're generally well-liked, you may receive invitations to participate in activities ranging from weddings to religious services to political meetings to sports events. Treat these invitations as honors or

tokens of respect. If the activity is to your taste, by all means take advantage of the invitation to learn more about the field site and to expand the perimeters of your life outside the narrow focus of your research. Be careful, though, that you as an outsider and a novelty do not become the focus of attention at the event, to the detriment of the people on whose behalf it is carried out. This is especially important for family events, such as weddings or funerals, when the family members should be the ones in the spotlight.

If, however, the invitation is for something that you don't want to do, such as to attend a religious service which is contrary to your own beliefs or a drinking party which you know will lead to unpleasant rowdiness, some creativity may be required. As with sex, outright refusal is usually not the best response. Coming up with a reason why you can't participate in the activity (not just a reason why you can't participate at this particular time) is usually a better strategy. Religious convictions are a good source of potential reasons to not participate, as are commitments to relatives or spouses back home and medical issues.

Lesson from the field:

A lot of people asked me to attend religious services with them, but I was not comfortable about this, because the services involved a lot of public profession of beliefs which I didn't hold. If I didn't make these professions, I'd feel obstructive and arrogant, but if I did participate, I'd feel like a hypocrite. I finally told the people who invited me that I was honoured by the invitation, but that the church I belonged to didn't take part in public prayers—we believed that spiritual relations should be a private matter between the individual and God, so we prayed alone. This answer got me off the hook without offending anyone, and it provided the answer to what my coworkers really wanted to know—whether I had any religious beliefs at all. I was a total atheist.

---

4. *Ongoing commitment to the community.* You may face requests for ongoing help to the community, even after you leave. While you may not be officially responsible for providing benefit to your site after the research is finished, this is an important ethical question nonetheless. One dimension of this question is reciprocity—if you have benefited from your fieldwork, whether in the form of receiving a higher academic degree, a salary, or valuable experience, you may consider yourself to have an obligation to reciprocate, with benefits for the people who helped you. In ideal circumstances, the research itself will have benefited the people in your field site, but this can't always be taken for granted, and the benefits may be quite abstract or quite minor compared with the very concrete gains you have received. Requests for ongoing involvement with the community can be seen as opportunities for reciprocation.

The other ethical dimension is that of broad redistributive justice. Especially if you are working in a community which is, on a global scale, poorer or more exploited than the one you come from, you may feel a responsibility to do your small part to redress the injustices which have given you advantages at the expense of others.

Lesson from the field:

Today I received a letter from a Chinese friend, written in green ink, which she explains is the color of love. She reminds me of the good times we had together in China, that she dreams of seeing us soon, and that we are her best friends. She closes her long, newsy, yet thoughtful letter with a request to come to my university and study with me—to be my PhD student. Yet my university has no PhD programs, nor do we offer a graduate degree in anthropology. I am at a loss as to the proper response. (Brewer 2006, 147)

These are all good reasons to maintain ongoing relations with the community in which you did your fieldwork, but you should be careful about the conduits which you use to contribute (even at the expense of some of your faith in human nature!). Can you be sure that the money, supplies, information or time that you provide will go to the people for whom it is intended, and not be siphoned off or redirected to others? Agreeing to maintain a relationship and flow of resources into a community is a responsibility, not just an act of kindness, and one aspect of that responsibility is making sure that those who should benefit are the ones who actually will benefit. (You should do some soul-searching to be sure that ongoing commitments you make are primarily for the benefit of the community, and not for your own ego [as a "benefactor"], or to smooth the way for further research.)

Ongoing commitments consisting of flows of money are the most liable to being diverted into other purposes—if you can, it's best to make commitments of other kinds. However, if you do want to continue a financial relationship, put some thought into how to facilitate the flow. One of the authors had a junior colleague in the field arrange to continue supporting the educational costs for a boy in the community, by giving money to a trusted friend and co-worker who would use the money to buy school supplies, supplementary books and other necessities for the boy, rather than giving it directly to the boy himself or his family, which would have subjected the boy to pressures to use the money to meet some of his family's other urgent needs.

Lesson from the field:

We met a woman at the clinic who had attended the same university that was sponsoring our project, and was excited to meet us. On the basis of this connection, she wanted to know if we would help to fund-raise at the university for a school for an orphanage she was trying to set up. On further discussion, however, it came out that this "school for orphans" was actually a private, fee-paying preschool for the children of the relatively well-off. Fund-raising for this venture would undoubtedly have increased this woman's business, and it may very well have been a good preschool, but it wouldn't have done anything for any orphans.

Finally, you should be sure that any commitments you make are ones which you can continue to honor into the indefinite future. This applies in small ways (giving people copies of pictures you have taken of them, for instance) as well as large. If you aren't sure whether you will have the resources or the will to keep honoring a commitment even after your vivid memories of the field fade, it's better not to commit, even at the cost of disappointing people who ask you for help.

Chapter 4

Establishing and Negotiating a Researcher Identity

For all the planning, organizing and work we do designing our projects, some things central to our research goals are well beyond our control. For instance, we can't ever completely control what other people think of us, which may not always tally with how we imagine ourselves. Our identities as individuals, researchers and community members will shape all aspects of the research process including the questions we choose to ask, how we design our study, how our participants perceive us, and the results. Thus, you need to think carefully about how to convey the person that you are. Doing so will help create a stronger research project, one that is more contextualized and situated.

Who Are You?[15]

Participants may have different views of the researcher than what the researcher believes he/she is projecting, especially when the researcher is participating in local activities. This discrepancy can create challenges regarding how the researcher identifies with participants and how participants interpret the researcher's behavior. The challenges of negotiating the "researcher role" continue even after the data-collection phase of fieldwork is over, as responsibilities to, and relationships with, participants shape the decisions researchers make when they analyze, write up and publish their work.

Sometimes the relationships between researchers and participants are characterized as one of either "outsiders" or "insiders," as though these two categories were opposites. These characterizations each come with ideas about the advantages and pitfalls of each type of position. Insiders may have more access to the information they need, developing trust and rapport with participants may be easier, and because they already understand the research topic or setting, they may be able to present a more complete picture of the phenomenon than their outsider colleagues. Outsiders may have the advantage of distance and perspective, they may be able to see things that an insider would not notice, and they can probe or uncover particular assumptions that both the insider researcher may share with research participants and thus never see.

So, while these roles can sometimes be viewed as opposing, they can both offer rich ways of understanding and researching a particular phenomenon. We can all gain a little insight into our field by asking how someone who is positioned differently to our field might approach the research and what they might see differently. Insiders may try to adopt a naïve approach and ask questions even when the answers may seem obvious. Outsiders may want to spend some time investing in the community to build the rapport (and thus benefit from both the insider and outsider perspectives), or outsiders may put conscious effort into looking for similarities with participants and finding ways to make connections.

Recently, this strict division of the researcher into either an insider or outsider has been questioned, and instead a more complex way of seeing these relationships is developing. In almost all research settings and with almost all research topics the researchers are often both inside and outside. These shifts between insider and outsider can happen in various ways in a project. Sometimes it is context dependent, thus that a researcher may feel like (or be) an insider in some contexts and an outsider in others,[16] or these perspectives may shift over time, so that a researcher could start out as an outsider and end up an insider.

You may also find that you're an outsider and an insider at the same time. For instance, a friend of Amy's was carrying out research on women's health in an area where she spoke the local language but was not a local resident. Coincidentally, she was also pregnant at the time. She found that her pregnancy gave her some instant commonalities with the women she was interviewing—they all sympathized with the minor physical discomforts of pregnancy, and were very interested in how she was feeling and whether the child would be a boy or a girl. Although she could never be as inside as someone who had grown up there, her pregnancy gave her an unexpected bridge to common experiences.

The ways that our identities impact and shape our research are multiple and complex. A researcher's identity involves a number of aspects, some of which the researcher may have some control over if and how to disclose, while others are immutable. Some of the most obvious identity characteristics are also some of our more important social markers: gender, race and/or ethnicity, age. Of course, these characteristics are difficult (although not entirely impossible) to change or conceal and are likely some of the first things that potential participants will notice. These characteristics can act as facilitators and inhibitors in the research process, and it is important to think about how they impact the creation of data. Would your participants have responded to you if you had been, say, female instead of male? Would a white researcher have had a different reception than a person of color?

Other identity characteristics also impact our research endeavors, but may be easier for the researcher to manage. Such characteristics may include religious affiliation, relationship status, whether the researcher has children, attitudes and beliefs, participation in certain activities and/or occupations. If, how and when these are disclosed are to a large degree at your discretion. Of course, researchers should be tuned in to any potential ethical dilemmas about disclosure or non-disclosure if such disclosure (or lack of disclosure) may leave participants feeling deceived or manipulated, versus when it allows the researcher his or her own privacy.

Here, we are not attempting to present a list of suggestions for ways to negotiate research relationships as they relate to identity. Instead we present a number of examples that highlight different issues around the topic of identity, to give you some ideas about things to think about throughout the research process.

Looks Can Be Deceiving

Often we assume that because we researchers share particular characteristics with our participants we are automatically insiders. The characteristics that help us to build rapport with participants will depend on the context of the study, such as the location and topic. Many times it is easiest for us to connect with people with whom we share important characteristics. It may be easier for women to open up to another woman interviewing them than a man (for example). However, our presumptions about our "insiderness" can be mistaken.[17]

Sometimes, social markers that align us with particular groups may not reflect the degree of insider or outsiderness felt in field settings. We may share characteristics with some of our participants, yet not share their world-view or their attitudes, making us outsiders as much as insiders. Similarly, we may feel alliances with those who would otherwise be considered outside our group.

In her fieldwork in San Francisco law firms, Jennifer Pierce describes two scenarios where her role as an insider or outsider was unexpected, and she highlights that it is sometimes other features that play a larger more important role in the development of connections and rapport with people. In the first instance, the researcher's identification as a feminist impeded her connection with other white female paralegals (a group with whom she belonged), while the way she behaved towards others created a stronger bond with someone who was less socially similar and with whom she may have assumed she would be more of an outsider (a Black female secretary).

Lesson from the field:

I encountered... obstacles to shared understanding in my interactions with a particular group of white female paralegals who were dubbed the "nicey-nice" women by their white male counterparts. As a white woman and as a paralegal, I qualified as an insider with respect to this occupational and racial/ethnic group. Yet as a feminist who viewed their submissive behavior critically, I felt like an outsider... . In supporting Kimberley's [a Black secretary in the law firm] personnel case, I became accepted as an ally against Princess Di [another white female paralegal in the office]. Her assertion that she liked the fact that I treated people as "just plain folks" suggests we also shared values about social etiquette. Still, her acknowledgement of "all that college education" and the repeated phrase "different for a white girl" served simultaneously to differentiate me from other white women in her eyes and to distinguish me from Black women. I felt not so much an insider... but an "outsider within." (Pierce 1995, 201-205)

Pierce's experience and the experiences of others serve as reminders that we must be careful when assuming that we share certain alliances or connections with particular research participants, or assume a lack of connection with others. It is inevitable that who we are, including the sex and race we were born into, will impact our research endeavors, but these impacts may take surprising and unexpected forms.

Assigned Identities

Our self-ascribed identities may be challenged in various ways throughout our everyday lives, but there is something about the process of research that sometimes has the effect of bringing issues of identity to the foreground. For instance, we often become so used to the ways we identify in our non-research setting that it can be quite startling when we realize that our research participants assign an identity to us that is not the way that we see ourselves.

Lesson from the field:

The people I lived with, those I went to the Buddhist temple with, and those I interviewed (the majority in the village) labeled me a farang [the term used for white people], something that rather shocked me. As an Asian, even as an Asian American, I had never seen myself as white. Now I was forced to view myself through the eyes of my informants as a farang, and to sort out what that identity meant. To be an Asian living in the United States meant being invested with the history, politics, and prosperity implied by the term "American." Yet, in my mind, ethnicity is very different from nationality. Living in America did not, therefore, qualify me as "white." In fact, my years in the United States have accentuated the differences between my ethnic identity and history and those of the "real" Americans I knew. (Fadzillah 2004, 40)

Fadzillah's experience is not uncommon for researchers of color when they venture into the field, especially when the field is a developing country. This can be true for people who were not born in the West (like Fadzillah) and who may experience life in the West as a "foreigner" to some degree (either because of language, or because they are not fully accepted). In a field setting, their alliance with a Western university can supersede the color of their skin (for example), and they can be classified as "white" despite their own ethnic identity.

This disconnection between a researcher's notion of his/her identity and the assumptions that participants make about a researcher are not limited to travels far from home. Although these disconnects are often not about broad identity issues such as race or gender, they may come in more subtle forms about assumptions regarding political affiliations, or attitudes toward a particular topic.

Lesson from the field:

Although most participants learned of Melanie's purpose for being in town quite quickly, they assumed that she went to the bar because she enjoyed hanging out and partying rather than as a means to recruit participants into the study. Many people mentioned that it was pretty "smart" of Melanie to manage to convince the university to pay for her to live in town for a summer and "conduct research." She was perceived primarily not as a researcher but, rather, as someone who went to the mountains to party and managed to do a little research on the side. This perception was useful to her as it enabled her to get into the scene of the seasonal workers and become accepted as part of the group. However, this perception also undermined perceptions of her qualifications and professionalism. Toward the end of the summer Melanie interviewed a woman with whom she had become acquainted through parties at the bars and other events. During the interview Melanie was asking many questions about hooking up and the bar scene in an effort to draw out this woman's reflections on casual sex. At one point the woman told Melanie that she should really start paying attention to this sort of behaviour while she was at the bar. Melanie was shocked, thinking "What do you think

I've been doing for the 6 weeks that I've been here already?" This incident was not the only time Melanie received comments that challenged her awareness of the processes of casual sex around her. (Lozanski and Beres 2007, 12)

Balancing Identities

In order to understand a particular experience, phenomenon or culture, many field researchers immerse themselves in their field and become part of the community. This might mean taking up a particular sport, activity or occupation, and it might mean learning something new, or returning to an already-familiar setting. For example Jennifer Pierce in the example above took a job as a paralegal in order to study workplace culture in law firms in the United States, while Rambo-Ronai took up a job as an exotic dancer while conducting an ethnography on the community of dancers. We all wear various hats throughout our lives and do not necessarily leave them all at home when we are doing our research. Some researchers, like the ones mentioned above, actively take on various hats as part of their research. This can lead to the necessity to balance these different hats and for the researcher to think about which hat is given priority at any one time.

Lesson from the field:

My ethnographic research examined the relationship between immigrant dance and ethnic construction. Through my fieldwork, I have realized the importance of embodied experience as a way of knowing, especially in a sociological research about dance. I enjoyed interacting with other dancers, and the vantage point of being part of the hustle and bustle in the dressing room before a big show opened, frantic yet methodic costume change in the hallway between dances, and shushed chit-chat while waiting behind the wings. Much of my data were collected in such exciting settings.

Embodiment, however, also posed problems. A good dancer is physically and mentally present. So is a good researcher. Can one be in one body, but with two different mind-sets simultaneously? The critical perspective I had developed through my research has shed new light on the dances we were doing, many of which were sexist or ethnocentric. I could no longer be fully present in the dances. As much as I needed to be there to get my data, being a half-hearted dancer was not enjoyable.

When I stopped dancing to focus on data analysis, I realized how deeply ingrained my identity as a dancer had become. I would dream about taking dance lessons and performing for months to come. I had "gone native"! I was blissfully spending more time studying and performing Chinese dance than writing my dissertation. Distance proved to be helpful as I re-anchored myself as a researcher. However, I went back to dance in the writing stage as I felt the need to reconnect my researcher-self and my dancer-self. I cannot produce knowledge about embodiment without being in my body, both as a dancer and as a sociologist.

While it can be tough to juggle these various hats and it can sometimes feel that you have a split personality, there are at times some ethical issues that need consideration. When we switch hats in the midst of research, participants may be confused or disturbed. For example, you may need both the self which is a sympathetic, compassionate listener and the self which is a dispassionate, data-hungry observer. If you are observing or interviewing people about volatile and emotionally-laden situations, such as the loss of a loved one, there may be times when the researcher-self thinks, "Wow! these are great data," while the compassionate self becomes aware that there are emotional needs which require attention and take precedence over gathering "great material." This might mean turning the tape-recorder off (literally and figuratively) in order to listen to a participant experiencing some emotional stress or pain. It could also mean tenuous and careful decisions about witnessing and/or disclosing illegal activities.

When Identities Collide

Researchers are sometimes faced with ethical dilemmas between doing what they think is right and potentially alienating a participant, or worse. At times these dilemmas may be anticipated; if I choose to study gang activities it is likely that I will witness some illegal activity, and I would likely think about this ahead of time. Other times we can be caught off guard by what we witness, and it can take us awhile to sort out what to do about this.

These dilemmas can be especially difficult for those researchers working with cultural groups with quite distinct values from their own. What is considered morally and ethically "right" in one context might be quite suspect in another. Researchers must be aware of the ways their own behavior is interpreted in addition to deciding how they will adapt to the setting within which they are doing research.

Some of these identity-related dilemmas include:

1. Being placed in an awkward position by different participants with competing goals. In any study there are bound to be multiple "stakeholders" whose goals are at times at odds with one another. As a researcher you may at times feel like you are being pulled into the debate and disagreement between stakeholders or that your research is being used to an end that you did not anticipate.

Lesson from the field:

Having recognized fairly early in my research that I was another of the principal's innovations, I slowly came to believe that Grace's initial call for me to present a "warts and all" picture of the school was not necessarily the straightforward granting of license I had imagined. I sensed that she was also extolling me to identify what needed changing, and to join her in the reform program, a positioning that I resisted as best I could. Given that Grace was my major sponsor, however, this was difficult to achieve in any direct way. Grace also endeavoured to position me as an assistant in her battle with the bureaucrats, whom she often spoke of in disparaging terms....

The discomfort I felt when one of the Ravina High's teachers suggested that I was "one of them" was an important moment in my research, one in which I was inadvertently called to return to the interstices. Given that I spent considerable amounts of time in the second half of the year moving among the teachers and recording their perspectives on what was happening to the school, it is easy to see why some assumed that I was aligned with those pitted against the principal. (Forsey 2004, 63-67)

Dealing with stakeholders with competing aims can be difficult. It is hard not to alienate either side, while also not taking sides or appearing too wishy-washy or uninterested. It could be tempting to avoid the situation all together and pull back, but the risk there is that you will automatically lose connections with people who could be potentially vital to your research aims. This requires that you weigh the benefits (or drawbacks) to your research and your research goals should you decide to distance yourself from one group of people or alienate them. As discussed in chapter 2, Drybread's decision to go to a judge to get her access to the prison reinstated was met with passive resistance by the prison administration who decided to enforce a policy that involved body searches upon her entry into the prison.

2. Forming alliances and friendships with participants that require collusion with lies or dishonest behavior. After spending considerable time in a research setting (or choosing to conduct research in a setting with which we are intimately familiar) it is reasonable to expect that you will not just be an objective observer, but that you will actually get to like some of your participants and become friends. These friendships have many benefits to the researcher, not the least of which is feeling less lonely in the field. Sometimes, these friendships may also stress our sense of what types of behavior we would normally engage in, and put us in unusual positions.

Lesson from the field:

Due to stigma, sex workers often keep their work a secret, especially from those closest to them. When outside the Zone, sex workers never refer to the place by name; rather they refer to it euphemistically as allá, or "there." As my relationship with the sex workers grew deeper and they invited me into their homes, I became responsible for maintaining their secrets, lying to their acquaintances and even to their children about how it was I came to know their mother or where I worked. Such lies produce a sense of alienation, create situations of inauthenticity in daily life, and are incredibly stressful to maintain. (Kelly 2004, 7)

These awkward situations could involve using drugs or alcohol in addition to lying or engaging in other forms of behaviour that we might not consider at home or outside of the research arena. It could also mean participating in spiritual or religious ceremonies we do not identify with. It is helpful to try and anticipate any of these situations ahead of time (religious affiliation, for example, may be an easier one to anticipate). But it is not possible to anticipate all possible dilemmas.

3. Remaining silent about issues of importance to ourselves. Sometimes researchers are drawn to a particular research topic because it has significance to them personally or professionally, and/or they may have particular views about issues related to their project. Running across participants who do not share your views is likely, and it is also quite possible that some participants might infuriate a researcher (and vice versa of course). With so much focus on developing a good relationship with participants it can feel very restrictive when we want to express a strong opinion related to something a participant has said.

Lesson from the field:

During the interview with Don about his casual sex experiences, I really found that my "feminist" brain was turned on. He seemed to have the whole "game" dialed and he knew exactly what he was doing and how get women to have sex with him. He also mentioned that sometimes a little coaxing was required. I asked him what he meant by coaxing—he said he would slow things down, or back up a little and then build up again when she is comfortable. I found myself wondering how those women felt, and what their perspectives on being "coaxed" were, I felt that his comments were disrespectful and potentially harmful toward women. At the same time I was trying to keep an open mind and make sure he felt that he was not being judged.

> *During the interview I felt torn between two directions. I want to listen to his perspective without judgment—to get a sense of where they are coming from and how they see the casual sex they are engaging in. I want him (and others) to feel relaxed enough to talk with me about casual sex. At the same time by staying silent when I hear comments that I find misogynist it seems to me like I am condoning or potentially reinforcing these negative and potentially dangerous ideas of women. I'm not sure how to balance this. I really wanted to tell him off, but is it better for me to listen with as little judgment as I can muster hoping that my analysis might shed some light on these issues in a constructive way?*

At these times it is helpful to think about the research goals both in terms of the particular project as well as the larger agenda, possibly including social change, of which your research is a part. The question then becomes one of how to best serve the goals of the broader agenda. In the example above Melanie decided that it was more helpful to stay silent and listen to Don's perspective (and similar perspectives from other men) than it was to resist and confront those participants. By listening Melanie developed a deeper analysis of these particular view points and may shed some light on additional ways to promote change.

These moments can be particularly painful when you are witness to participants' views about some characteristic which is central to your own sense of identity. Listening to disturbing opinions about race, sexuality or gender, for instance, may make you feel as though a yawning gap has just opened up. In these cases, it's important to have some sort of "safe space" outside the research where you can acknowledge these disturbing experiences and restore your sense of self. A friend you can write to, a place you can visit, or even a journal where you can vent your distress without self-censorship are examples of such safe spaces.

Of course there are times when it may be quite appropriate and reasonable to challenge participants on their views in the same way one might challenge a colleague or friend who says something with which we disagree. There may be ways we can challenge participants constructively that could lead to discussion of an issue and a better understanding of the participant's perspective.

Shifting Identities

Often when we think about research and our identities, the first thoughts that come to mind are how our identities shape the research project and (potentially) the participants. In particular when we address research ethics we are required to think about the potential harms and benefits of participating in research—essentially, how the research could change the people who choose to participate in it. But the participants are not the only ones who risk change (for better or worse) as they involve themselves with the research project. Researchers themselves often leave a field site or wrap up a project thinking differently about issues related to their research, or otherwise altered from where they began.

This feeling of being "changed" by experiences can take the form of reverse culture shock, in which returning to a once-familiar environment—your home—can be as stressful as leaving that home was in the first place. Many of us who have done extended stints overseas can testify to the unexpected strength of reverse culture shock. However, this phenomenon isn't limited to people who travel across the world to do their fieldwork. Even if your field is just a few blocks from your apartment, the beliefs, values and ideas of the field which you have been working so hard to understand may have taken up permanent residence in your psyche, and may be hard to leave behind. Don't be distressed if you find that your "field self" doesn't stay in the field, but comes back with you when your fieldwork is over. The reactions to your home environment that you experience as a result of your field experience can tell you some valuable things about the field, even if you only really become aware of these reactions after you go home.

Lesson from the field:

I sat alone during supper at the lodge, nursing my quarter grilled chicken and rice as I read my book. Frankee, the lodge's Assistant Manager, entered the kitchen from the back door and sat down across from me. His speech was slurred and he was noticeably drunk. As I answered his many questions about why I was alone that night, he asked me if I had a fiancé. I told him 'no'. I thought his eyes were going to bust from their beds in disbelief. He told me that he was "forced" to get married, and explains that in Malawi, people think there is something wrong with you if you are not married by a certain age. He then says, "the problem here [in Malawi] is AIDS", and points his finger in the direction of the notorious Riverside Bar across the way from the lodge. He says that the "bitches" [sex workers] there will do anything for money. He then tells me that he himself is HIV positive and all he does is drink beer and stay faithful to his wife. He invites me to join him for a beer. I decline politely. As a moment of silence approaches, I tell him that my stomach is upsetting me and that I am going to return to my room and go to sleep. I went back in my room that night and sat on my bed in absolute silence. I couldn't read. I had no motivation to watch a DVD, especially since my collection was limited to 'Sex in the City', tales that emerge from places where wealth is ubiquitous and sex, for some at least, less punitive. At that moment, the reality of my research was catching up with me for the first time. And all I could do was cry.

Chapter 5

Gathering Data

Beginning researchers must first come to terms with the possibility that their work, like all field research, may be to some degree a failure. This is not to say that fieldwork is pointless, but the research design for fieldwork that can be relied on to produce completely objective, exhaustive and fully verifiable knowledge about any question in the social sciences has not yet been created.

Scholars in some disciplines, such as anthropology or sociology, have come to terms with the impossibility of finding "the truth" or "the answer" to a research question, and argue that the researcher's job is to produce a logical, well-thought-out and honest representation of reality as the researcher encounters it. Other disciplines, such as political science and economics, still retain the older epistemological faith that with adequate rigor, perfectly factual and unbiased information can be retrieved from fieldwork. However, given the many points of view from which any social phenomenon can be viewed, as well as the difficulty of ever escaping completely from one's own biases and preconceptions, we believe that the former approach to research is more consistent with fieldworkers' actual experiences.

Most research plans, prepared before heading into the field, are detailed, well-thought-through and well-written, conforming to institutional requirements as well as to the researcher's commitment to problem-solving and the creation of new knowledge. Looking back from the perspective of a completed project, however, most research plans are works of fiction, describing the researchers' hopes, rather than predicting what ended up happening. Data collection in the field often looks quite different from the way it looked in the planning stage of the research. Unanticipated difficulties emerge, but unanticipated opportunities also arise. The intent of this chapter is to help researchers minimize the possibility of being defeated by common challenges in data gathering, as well as to help researchers seize on the unanticipated opportunities to improve and strengthen their research, beyond what was envisioned in their plan.

Lesson from the field:

Overall, my experience in the field implementing the research memorandum I designed while still in the U.S. would appear as a failed effort. Because of time constraints associated with my involvement with a greater data collection project, and my overestimation of my availability at the conclusion of working for that project, I was never able to schedule or conduct interviews in the capital city. My research at the local-level was also never completely implemented. The benefit, however, of being part of a large group of collaborative researchers was that colleagues were more than willing to share any data they had gathered, including transcripts of interviews. The research design I crafted in the states was too ambitious an undertaking to carry out while also committing to work for a large-scale survey project, especially when I was generating and exploring new research ideas in the field.

Preparation and Flexibility

Given that fieldwork rarely maps perfectly onto research plans, researchers need to be prepared for plans to change. Reflexivity, in the form of willingness to think critically about your own data collection, is crucial, as is flexibility, in the form of readiness to change what doesn't work. Some epistemological paradigms encourage reflexivity and flexibility, such as grounded theory, with its emphasis on continuous reflection.[18] Others, such as positivism, have historically been less ready to accept the indeterminacy of research. We believe that researchers need to be prepared to change when the situation calls for it—it's better to change horses in midstream than to keep going doggedly despite mounting difficulties and suspicions that the data you're collecting may not be as useful as you want them to be.

> *Lesson from the field:*
>
> *During the first day of data collection, one of our best interviewers made a serious mistake. A mixed-methods endeavor, our protocol involved conducting an in-depth interview, after which time the quantitative data would be collected quickly, using a structured questionnaire. One interviewer had other plans. He came back from his first day in the field having executed the questionnaire first because it "made more sense." "But we had a protocol!" "But it was easy to lead with the questionnaire." "But we have a protocol. We gather the qualitative data first!" The argument was resolved when a colleague rightly noted: "This, my friends, is an empirical question." An empirical question it was, and we proceeded to design a methodological experiment to determine the differences in administering a survey prior to an in-depth interview or vice-versa.... Findings: Conducting the in-depth interview prior to the*

> *structured questionnaire was, indeed, the preferable order for our particular topics of inquiry. The language of these respondents was more spontaneous. These interviews were longer and spent more time covering topics we considered "sensitive." But we wouldn't have known empirically this was the case if not for our interviewer's early mistake.*

To minimize unexpected surprises in the field, you should do as much preparatory work as possible while still at home, whether home is a geographical location or a phase of research. If you're leaving for a new location, find out as much as you can about your field site in advance, from the obvious sources (Google, guidebooks) and the not-so-obvious ones (online versions of local newspapers, chat groups for people living in the area). If possible, meet with people who are from your field site before you leave, to get a less formal perspective on what it will be like to do research there. Be aware, though, that the expatriates you meet may have their own particular point of view about their homeland, and may not be representative of the majority of the population.

Gather this information with an eye to how it might affect the logistics of collecting your data—for instance, if you're traveling to a part of the world that has a monsoon cycle, at what point in the cycle will you be there? How might the weather affect plans to, for instance, distribute a survey across a wide area? If you will need to be in contact with colleagues back home, how reliable are phone services? Are Internet cafes hard to find? Bear in mind the timing of fieldwork in terms of local political, economic and agricultural cycles. These can be crucial to its success. For instance, you might not want to carry out interviews on politically sensitive issues in the midst of a hotly-contested election campaign.

Lesson from the field:

A Masters student studying urban governance in Dhaka conducted fieldwork in Bangladesh during Ramadan in 2001. While time constraints meant this was unavoidable and provided challenges, field-work was still possible. In particular, it meant conducting interviews very early in the morning before people became tired, and eating discretely in her hotel room during the day. Most offices closed at 3 p.m. which meant that the latest possible interview time was 1 or 2 p.m. Because of traffic congestion (which worsened during Ramadan), it was rarely possible to conduct more than two interviews per day. While this provided obvious limitations, it also gave the researcher a greater appreciation of the difficulties of conducting business and government during the Muslim month of fasting than would have been the case had she avoided it. (Scheyvens and Nowak 2006, 91)

Pre-fieldwork preparation includes familiarizing yourself with the methods you intend to use, as well as familiarizing yourself with the site. If you intend to embark on a project using methods you've never used before, or never used outside the classroom, getting some real-world experience will help to avoid unpleasant surprises once you actually try to carry out your own sample survey, or conduct your own focus groups or lead your own social mapping exercise, as the case may be. In order to gain this experience, consider doing a formal or informal practicum with someone who is already using the methods you want to use. Interning on someone else's project can give you a feel for what you will be doing, with no risk to your own research enterprise.

At the very least, you should try to get access to raw data generated by the method you intend to use, rather than only polished, written-up accounts of research. Seeing the actual maps created from a social mapping exercise in participatory research or reading the verbatim transcripts of open-ended interviews may alert you to potential issues you may face once you start generating your own social maps and interview transcripts.

As the beginning of fieldwork approaches and you're thinking more about the nitty-gritty of what to bring, try to maximize self-reliance. The less you have to depend on other people to get through a day of fieldwork, the fewer surprises you will have. For instance, if you are receiving financial support for your fieldwork, try to arrange that you yourself are the one who will be receiving and managing the funds, rather than routing them through a third party such as a partner organization. Similarly, if you need the help of research assistants, it's better to try to arrange to employ a smaller number of RAs who are working exclusively through you rather than sharing a larger workforce with another researcher.

Be aware, though, that there are situations in which excessive self-reliance and independence could be injurious to the social relations you develop with the community in which you are working—for instance, eating only food you brought with you could be seen as stand-offish, as could your reliance on music, books and entertainment you bring from home. However, when it comes to the actual mechanics of gathering data, self-reliance is best. In practical terms, this means bringing extras of everything essential to your work. If you are doing interviews, bring an extra digital recorder or tape recorder; if you are carrying out surveys, print out more copies than you think you will need. Make multiple photocopies of your passport (if needed) and any other documentation which authorizes you to be doing what you're doing. The same principle applies to research time—plan to spend more time in the data gathering phase of research than you think you'll need, and allow yourself extra time for any travel.

Along the same lines, make arrangements for backup copies of all the data you collect in the field. You should be sure you have all your data in at least two places—on a laptop and backed up on a USB drive, for instance, or on two different desktops, or in written form and digital form. Some fieldworkers with Internet access email their notes and transcripts to a friend or colleague at home. (Be sure you follow standards of anonymity and confidentiality if you choose this route.) One of the authors went to graduate school with a fellow student who carried out an ambitious three-country comparative study of business and corporate culture—and then had his laptop stolen from an airport, losing all the data he had amassed.

The ultimate form of preparation is the pilot study—a sort of dress rehearsal for the actual research to come, in which you apply your research design in a trial setting. Whenever possible, try to pilot your project on a small scale before leaping into it wholesale. (Be sure not to mix up your data from the pilot study, when you will still be working out the kinks in the research plan, with your data from the "real" research.) However, most people don't have the time or the resources to thoroughly pilot everything. The section below deals with some of the most common problems that crop up in fieldwork, becoming evident only once your research has begun.

Unexpected, but Not Uncommon, Roadblocks in Data Collection

The following are some of the more common challenges that fieldworkers encounter in collecting data. Other types of challenges are specific to specific methodologies, such as participant observation or surveys. We are presenting these challenges here not to provide strict guidelines on how to deal with them, but to give you an idea of situations you might need to work through.

1. *Surprise! You realize that your research question is unanswerable.* You may have come to the field with a research question or hypothesis which is eminently logical in the context of existing literature, only to discover that you are not

able to answer it. Sometimes this is due to logistical problems, lack of resources while in the field, or lack of time. However, sometimes the unanswerability of research questions can be traced to less obvious social and cultural factors. One example is the local notion of what constitutes "sensitive" or "taboo" subject matter. You may want to find out about sexual practices, to take an obvious example, but discover that talking about such matters, or talking honestly, with a stranger is considered unacceptable by your respondents. Another common "taboo" is discussion of individual wealth or resources. You may want to carry out a household survey of assets, but revealing the extent of one's wealth is considered too sensitive, especially if respondents think this information might find its way into the hands of tax collectors or other government officials. Personal unhappiness and experiences of violence are other examples of areas in which research questions may prove to be unanswerable.

It's important to attend to cues in your daily research work indicating that respondents are not comfortable providing information, such as potential respondents avoiding you or your RAs, or providing only vague and minimal information. These are signs that your question may not be answerable in the context and with the methodologies that you have at your disposal, and that the information you do manage to obtain may not be valid.

Lesson from the field:

I sat in an immaculate office in the Rwandan capital Kigali with a bureaucrat who crossed out words on my questionnaire with a black bic pen. "Your research team cannot ask about ethnic groups' " he dug the pen into the paper. I sighed inwardly, but this was the expected response. I wasn't an independent researcher who could slip under the government radar, I was working with a registered NGO. Then, could I use the word "group" in general? I felt confident my participants would understand the implication of group as ethnic. "No", the bureaucrat shook his head. "You can't use the word 'group'." I started to fidget. I was supposed to research ethnic relations without using the word "ethnic" or "group." "What word do you suggest, then?" He tapped his pen against my questionnaire. "Perhaps, 'people'. For example in question number 15, 'I would be willing to allow my daughter to marry 'people'." Later that day my Rwandan research assistant spoke in low consoling tones. "We will write 'people' and say "people" but as we explain the question, participants will understand what we mean. Everyone speaks in code here." Recent arrests of Rwandan researchers working for an international organization weighed on my mind. "But if this code is so easy to understand, what is the difference? Aren't our researchers still at risk for discussing ethnicity?" He shrugged. "Our participants know us, so I don't think there will be a problem. And I don't think we have another choice." (Paluck 2007, 3)

Another reason why your research plans may not be viable is that you may not be able to gain access to the people who have the information that you're seeking. Your own (or your RAs') gender, age, ethnicity and social position may influence who will or won't disclose information to you. For example, if a male researcher wanted to learn about subsistence farming in parts of Africa, he might have a very difficult time getting access to the people who actually know the most about it—female peasant farmers. You can also find your access to information blocked when the people in the know consider you or your RAs too old, too young, too male, too female, too wealthy, too poor, too different or too familiar to talk to.

Lesson from the field:

[The respondent] seemed nervous although the interview was in her place so I asked if she would like somebody to sit in with us. She agreed and a man came in, we explained what we were doing and it went well until the husband came in about half way through the interview. He had a very pissed off look on his face. I tried to explain my research, he sat and shortly left. He didn't seem to understand my explanation, asking aggressively why we wanted to know this information..... He comes back in after five minutes and asks how long we'll be. I have more than half an hour of questions I'd like to cover, but cut my estimate to say, 'I'll only be 5 or 10 minutes if that's OK with you'. He wants to talk with her for 5 minutes and they leave. I'm nervous this big man might come flying in with fists of fury and [my research assistant] Chris and I plan our escape if it comes to pulling a runner. She comes back, a little shaken, and I keep strictly to my self-imposed ten minute deadline, fearful of Mike Tyson in the red corner. Lesson? We'd been invited into her place by her, in the absence of her husband. Didn't think of asking his permission since he wasn't there at the time—previous interviews were either with men, or women who we interviewed at or near their business location, not at home. We never found out why. Because we were in his house, interviewing his wife without his permission? The content of the interview?—being her business affairs? Him not getting any (immediate?) benefit from the interview (of his wife)? He asked us when leaving how we would come back to help with the information I'd stolen from his wife. 'You'll never return here', he said."

2. *Surprise! Your methodology doesn't work for your research question.* Some researchers go into the field firmly committed to a particular way of gathering knowledge, whether because they have been schooled in this particular way or because they have always done things this way and have not thought about changing. However, the lack of fit between research methods and research goals may not be evident until you actually begin working.

This is particularly the case when researchers attempt to answer questions most suited to qualitative (subjective, inductive, intensive, small number of cases) research questions with methods suited to quantitative questions (objective, deductive, extensive, large number of cases), or vice versa. You should be willing to question the fit between the data and your research question constantly, as you gather the data. You may find that you have gathered data on one aspect of the topic you are studying, but not the aspect that you wanted (or promised) to investigate. For instance, attempting to study demand for child care through qualitative interviews with a small group of parents may give you information on the strategies people use to find care for their children, or their feeling about the lack of good child care, but won't give you information adequate to forecast the community-level demands for such care, if that were your original question.

Lesson from the field:

First, there were problems with obtaining the 'random' sample hoped for. A number of "gatekeepers" had to be relied on for contacts within the communities. Clearly, this led to a bias, as the individuals would select those who they felt would be 'most interested' and 'interesting'. Second, the postal questionnaire was a failure (three responses from thirty; two of which were to inform me that they couldn't help!). Personal, pre-appointed visits were the only way that the export companies could be successfully approached, which all took time. Third, it was time consuming to track down individuals. The growers' work took place from sun-up until sun-down. More often than not I would attempt to locate them at their plots (parcelas) and these parcelas were sometimes very far apart... .Riding up to 50 km in the Chilean sun on mainly rough stone surface roads and with pockets full of stones to scare off mad dogs, was not envisaged during the research design phase. (Donovan and Storey 2006, 34)

If you encounter such a mismatch between data and methods, you have essentially three options: give up altogether (not recommended); change your methodology to fit your research question (possible if you realize the lack of fit between question and methods early enough in the fieldwork stage) or retrofit your research question so it corresponds more closely to the data that you obtain (this is the least desirable, since you presumably chose your original research question for specific reasons, but it's better than ending up drawing conclusions of questionable validity).

3. *Surprise! Conditions in the field are such that your research can't proceed as planned.* Some field conditions can be anticipated by careful study of the field site before you begin, as recommended above; however, other conditions may arise as you work. For instance, changes in the level of personal risk of danger may make it less than prudent to keep going if, say, political violence intensifies or an economic collapse occurs. A common form of changes in the field is when resources (human and material) that you were counting on aren't there, or disappear. A key contact person who could open the door to a community moves away, for instance, or promised institutional support is not adequate for the demands you make on

it, or costs prove to be much higher than you expected. Again, as suggested above, doing detailed research before beginning your fieldwork and prioritizing self-reliance in your preparations can help to minimize the risk of unexpected field conditions, but nothing can eliminate this risk.

Lesson from the field:

Most NGOs are not prepared to handle the sudden spike in demand for logistical support created by a research project and the accompanying research team. A collaborating researcher should be prepared to act as a logistician, accountant, mediator, shopper, and even chauffeur—all roles that I assumed in order to realize the fieldwork plans. I learned NGO organizational language and procedure, "foreign" words like proforma and ordre de mission, acronyms like MOU and TOR, and mastered dozens of forms, contracts, and banking regulations. I was often called on to intervene in salary negotiations and advances for my researchers, discussions about car drivers and mechanical problems and office politics. (Paluck 2007, 16)

4. *Surprise! Your data don't appear to make any sense.* Most fieldworkers have had the experience of being confronted, mid-project, with the suspicion that they are really not learning what they want, or that their data will never add up to any important or useful conclusions. This experience is more common among researchers using inductive epistemologies, such as grounded theory, as distinct from deductive epistemologies, such as hypothesis-testing. Inductive methodologies encourage researchers to develop frameworks for analyzing the data in tandem with the collection of data, an approach that has much to commend it, but one which can also lead to

frustrations when your data don't seem to be giving you anything to build an analytical framework from.

One common cause of this frustration is theorizing in advance of data collection—that is, trying to understand a phenomenon or explain occurrences before you have sufficient data to use as grist for your analytical mill. If you experience this sinking feeling early in the process of fieldwork, wait until you have collected more data before you start to panic. Some researchers make it a point of not looking at their data until at least half of it has been obtained, or until they have enough data for patterns to emerge. The first few interviews or surveys or focus groups or maps or ethnographic observations may or may not be representative of broader patterns to come, so don't expect yourself to have things figured out early on, and don't let your early results shape your expectations of what may emerge from your later results.

In some cases, again particularly when using inductive methodologies, the really important findings may not become clear to you until after you leave the field and have time to sit back and look at your data as a whole, rather than trying to coordinate data collection with analysis. Patterns often become much clearer with hindsight, even though you may be left wishing you could go back and do your fieldwork over again, to bring out more details of the patterns you've discovered.

Lesson from the field:

During the third interview for my dissertation research, I was introduced to two concepts by [an interview participant]: chivanhu, which can be roughly translated as the way of the people or indigenous ways; and chirungu, meaning English, European, or modern ways. Then in her late 70s, Louise was excited about the opportunity to tell her life story.... She used the ideas of chivanhu and chirungu to frame her personal history, explaining that when she was a child people in her part of the country followed indigenous ways, which were marked by limited wants that could be met from local resources . ... However, people had slowly been drawn to chirungu over her lifetime, lured by the promise of new kinds of goods such as clothes and dishes, money to pay for them, and the necessity of waged work or crop sales to earn those funds. ...While I had enjoyed the interview... I was puzzled and somewhat discouraged. I was worried I would never be able to direct people to the topics that really interested me, primarily how people in the area had resisted government efforts to direct land use and farming practices. Almost two years later, I was struggling. I had a solid, but dull chapter drawing entirely on archival material to explain why government efforts to reshape rural people's livelihoods increased so dramatically after the Second World War. ... My advisor read the chapter, and asked why I thought this was the first chapter, when I had such rich material on people's lives, social arrangements, and farming practices. It took me a while to think it through, but I then decided to foreground the material coming out of the interviews, and what I had imagined as ten pages of background material in the third chapter morphed into the first two and half chapters. ... I began to see ongoing debates about the past and its implications for the present. I wished I had spent more time exploring the nuances of people's opinions, or had gotten several people together to debate the implications of chirungu and chivanhu—but that left me with intriguing research possibilities once I finished my PhD.

---

5. *Surprise! The information you gather is distorted by the data collection method itself.* This is a very common form of validity problem, yet one which often goes unrecognized in the articles, theses, books and reports which emerge from much fieldwork. Social scientists know this as the Hawthorne effect, occurring when behaviors under study (including responding to surveys, participating in interviews, or otherwise providing direct information) are altered by the fact that they are being studied. The result is the provision of biased information, which may or may not reflect the respondent's actual experience.

For instance, in studies of sexual behavior, people may acknowledge fewer sexual partners than they have actually had, because they don't wish to appear "promiscuous" in the eyes of the interviewer. Similarly, a focus group on a particular topic may produce a false impression of consensus on that topic, because dissenters may not want to reveal themselves as having contrary opinions. You should always approach your data with a skeptical eye, asking yourself "what reasons might respondents have had for giving the answers that they did? What other interests or agendas might be at work here?" This is not to suggest that your participants routinely lie or provide dishonest information, but to recognize that there is always much more going on in any information-gathering project than meets the eye.

Simple courtesy may lead to distortions in the information provided, as respondents tell researchers what they think the researchers want to hear, as in studies of condom use in high-HIV prevalence communities, which appeared to show that everyone in the community had positive attitudes towards condom use, when in fact respondents were providing answers which they thought the interviewers would regard as "good", rather than accurate answers about their attitudes. This sort of effect can also come about as a result of expectations for what may follow the research project—for instance,

Amy had the experience of people overstating their lack of assets in a household survey, in the hopes that the research project was paving the way for economic assistance based on need.

Lesson from the field:

I was suspected by members of an informal construction worker (ICW) group on the outskirts of Dar es Salaam, of conducting a feasibility study for a United Nations agency. Two group members aggressively demanded to know how my organisation was going to finance them, and this is after I made it very clear that I was not working with the United Nations and had only got their details from the United Nations 'Support for Informal Construction Workers in Dar es Salaam' ('STICW-Dar es Salaam') project. This situation was perhaps the most difficult to negotiate during the 18 months of fieldwork since it was most obvious to me then that I had failed in my efforts to express that my research was my own. It was also then that it most struck home that, as with most academic studies, it is the researcher who benefits from the research, however well-meaning otherwise.

All of the above surprises speak to the importance of always having a Plan B (or C, or D). Rigidity in the face of the ever-changing and ever-surprising conditions of fieldwork is a great danger for any research project. Research projects can fail if the people doing the research lack either the perceptiveness to notice that something is going wrong in their data collection, or the imagination to come up with ways to counter this. Unexpected challenges in data collection are not a sign that your plans were inadequate or your project is doomed, but they can be an opportunity for you to develop and flex your fieldwork skills.

Lesson from the field:

A number of positive 'chance' discoveries also partly altered the direction of research. For example, whilst in a legal office in [a major market town] for another purpose, a large set of fruit sale contracts drawn up between export firms and farmers was stumbled upon. The analysis of these contracts formed a major section in the final thesis. Surprise meetings with informed individuals also became increasingly important. A chance meeting occurred in a restaurant with [a lawyer], somebody who had worked in the defense of small farmers in disputes concerning the re-possession of their property by companies. Further meetings helped clarify the aims and objectives of the project in an important way. Of course, in cases where chance discoveries are made, one often has to rapidly alter tack and not become excessively concerned if the research timetable is altered. (Donovan and Storey 2006, 37)

One excellent tool for enhancing your flexibility is the fieldwork journal. For ethnographers, keeping such a journal, or field notes, is an essential tool for their work, but even if you are not embarked on ethnography, a field journal in which you record your observations, decisions, and evolving understandings of the field can be invaluable.[19] The journal can serve as a record of decisions made on the fly in the fluid, rapidly-changing fieldwork environment, and can remind you of the contexts behind any decisions you need to make. Fieldwork journals can also be great resources once you stop collecting data and start devoting your time to making sense out of it.

Chapter 6

Research Ethics

The central idea of research ethics—that research should be done in a way that's consistent with some objective idea of right or wrong conduct—is extraordinarily broad. In practice, when people talk about research ethics, they usually mean one of three things: one of two more philosophical interpretations of ethics; or the administrative and bureaucratic requirements for you to get "ethics approval" for a proposed project. In this chapter, we will discuss each of these three meanings of ethics.

The two most prominent philosophical orientations to ethics include the idea that one should do no harm in the course of research, and the idea that one should go beyond just doing no harm, and should actively try to do good in the course of research. We will call these two interpretations *"minimalist ethics"* and *"maximalist ethics."* Each of these interpretations of ethics imposes responsibilities on you as a researcher. How you choose to interpret these responsibilities, and what you intend to do to meet (or ignore) them is up to you. In this chapter, we provide a quick guide to some of the things you might take into consideration.

Minimalist Ethics

This ethical stance holds that the primary responsibility of the researcher is to avoid doing harm—to be ethically neutral. At first glance, the idea that fieldwork could actually be harmful may seem unlikely. Social scientists don't make weapons or pollutants, and they don't carry out risky or experimental medical procedures. However, every entry into a preexisting and emergent social situation—the essence of fieldwork—will alter that situation, for better or for worse. Almost everyone adheres to this minimal standard of ethics, in that no one sets out on fieldwork intending to mess up the lives of their participants, but it's easy to unintentionally do harm.[20]

One form of unintentional harm is offending existing norms. Fieldworkers who are going far from home should think about their self-presentation—clothing, deportment, conversation—and whether it will be consistent with existing norms for people of their gender and age in the community where they are working.[21] Those who are doing research "at home" can also face those dilemmas, but in a less powerful fashion. Sometimes, bringing oneself into consistency with existing norms can be as simple as not wearing sleeveless shirts or not using coarse language; but at other times, the work of fitting in may require more radical alterations of self, such as not speaking in the presence of the other gender or professing nonexistent religious beliefs.

For some researchers, the cost of fitting in, in terms of personal integrity ("being myself") and in terms of supporting norms which the researchers may find objectionable, is too high. If that's the case for you, you may risk doing a little harm by offending people, rather than committing what you see as the greater harm of being untrue to yourself and your values. This in itself is an ethical choice, and if this choice is not made consciously, you may find yourself uncomfortable or resentful about the differences between your own standards of conduct and the ones prevalent in your study community.

Lesson from the field:

What is protection and what is harm? Certainly writing anything or acting in any way that will bring a people undesired attention from repressive or extractive state bureaucracies is harm, as is raising false expectations or promising the undeliverable, or conducting questioning that is in any way coerced or uncomfortable for them. ... At present, many villagers in Liangshan do not clearly understand the purpose of fieldwork and even if they did understand it and approve of it now, what will they think in 20 years or the next generation? Would they feel better if they were anonymous, or would they rather see their names in print, especially if the latter caused the writer to be more careful about what he wrote? (Ayi, Harrell and Lunzy 2007,297)

Another form of unintentional harm is demands on participants' resources, both tangible and intangible. Participants' tangible resources may include food, transport, accommodation and other sorts of sustenance, which they generally need more than you do. Most researchers would never ask a participant to feed or house them, but the issue becomes more difficult if participants offer out of personal generosity or out of adherence to community norms of hospitality. Even if the participant is wealthier than you are, accepting anything is potentially awkward and should be avoided if possible, unless refusal would give grave offense. In those situations where you can't refuse, finding a way to reciprocate is the best course to take, so as not to become a drain on participants or to become indebted to them in a way which might influence the course of your work.

Lesson from the field:

Bartolo began making demands on me that I was unsure about. By this time he had more than demonstrated his friendship, but there were disquieting aspects about our relationship that I did not know how to interpret ... "Compadre, my family would like a television set."

"You want a gift?" I said, taken aback.

"They all want to watch television here in the house," he replied.

... I was uneasy about the effect television would have on village life. What changes would it bring? Would it raise unrealistic expectations? ... Stalling for time, I answered, "Compadre, I don't have to tell you that watching television is a waste of time. You have seen it before. People just sit for hours and watch and don't get any work done. Are you sure this is a good idea?"

He paused a moment and said "Yes, compadre, they want it."...

I told Bartolo, "Let me think about it." (Sandstrom 2006, 20)

One resource that is often unintentionally exploited is time. Most researchers would not dream of asking a participant to give them his/her car or bank account numbers, but we often fail to realize that time is a valuable commodity for participants, too. In order to do minimal harm, researchers should be aware of the opportunity costs of participating in the research—by agreeing to take part in an interview, survey or other data-collection exercise, what opportunities is the participant foregoing? What would s/he be doing with his/her time if not talking to you? Minimizing the time demands of research by being as parsimonious as possible in designing surveys or interview guides is an important but often overlooked dimension of ethics.

Lesson from the field:

I was working on a project which had a household survey as one component. The survey was long and complicated. It had lots of skip patterns and required intricate, detailed answers for some questions. It also had to be repeated every six months, according to the study design. The participants hated answering the survey. They were willing to do it the first time, but when we tried to do the follow-ups they would pretend not to be home, or would say they had to leave and go somewhere urgently. If they couldn't get out of it, they picked the quickest and most superficial answers to the questions. I believe they were protecting their time against our demands for it, and I really wonder about the data quality of that survey.

Another intangible resource is participants' psychological well-being. To avoid doing harm here, you should do your best to ensure that your research does not become a source of psychological stress from uncertainty or worry. This means being as transparent as possible in explaining the motives, methods and end products of your project, to dispel any mystery or confusion. It also entails doing your best not to raise false hopes about the outcomes of the project, to avoid the harm of disappointment.[22]

Sometimes, this aspect of not doing harm may mean that you need to redefine, or even abandon, a particular direction in your research, if you discover that the topics which you want to find out about are distressing to the participants to recount. Such topics might include violence, experiences of trauma, sexual activities, or loss and grief.[23] Interview guides and surveys should be structured so that participants have an "out", to avoid feeling that they have to relive painful experiences for the benefit of the researcher. In carrying out research on topics that might be sensitive, you should remain constantly alert for signs of distress or discomfort among participants, especially in cross-cultural contexts where the cues may not be easy for you to pick up.

Lesson from the field:

One of the key areas I wanted to explore concerned how people had resisted government efforts to direct land use and farming practices. ...I assumed peasants in the area where I was working would be willing, if not eager, to discuss political agitation, the protests, and the acts of sabotage. ...However, as I began interviewing people, they denied these events took place, or simply refused to speak about them. Puzzled, I tried a range of strategies—opening by talking about the protests, or only asking questions about them after an hour or so of discussing social change, farming practices and other matters, or raising the idea when I first discussed my research interests with interviewees. Yet the silences continued, and I finally began to understand why in an interview with a man in his sixties who had a very sharp memory. As we went through questions about his life, he spoke willingly and with a great deal of enthusiasm, even providing dates that matched ones I had come across in the government archives. I was excited as we moved to discussing the protests, but after I asked my first question, he looked me directly in the eyes and said: "It is too long ago, I don't remember." I was chilled by his reply, dropped the topic, and shifted to asking about social dynamics and farming practices. We continued to have a lively conversation, and seemed to part on good terms.

As I reflected on this interview and the wider silences about the protests, I knew I had been asking about an area that was too sensitive for many people to discuss.

The potential for harm may continue even after the research in the field has ended. In the ways that your work is written up, presented, and disseminated, negative stereotypes about groups of people may be inadvertently reinforced, particularly if you are working in a community which is already subject to stigma.[24] You may be torn between presenting their data accurately and protecting the reputation of your participants from being tarnished, especially if you personally sympathize with the people you worked with. In such cases, you may find yourself torn between loyalty to your data and to the goals of disinterested scholarship, and loyalty to the people with whom you worked.

Lesson from the field:

What do we do with information about the ways in which women on welfare virtually have to become welfare cheats ... to survive? A few use more drugs than we wish to know; most are wonderful parents but some underattend to their children well beyond neglect. These are the dramatic consequences, and perhaps also the "facilitators" of hard economic times. To ignore the data is to deny the effects. To report the data is to risk their likely misinterpretation. How do we connect troubling social/familial patterns with macrostructural shifts when our informants expressly don't make the connections? ...With data collection over and analysis now under way, we continue to struggle with how best to represent treacherous data—data that may do more damage than good, depending on who consumes/exploits them, data about the adult consequences of child physical

> *and sexual abuse, data suggesting that it is almost impossible to live exclusively on welfare payments (encouraging many to lie about their incomes so that they feel they are welfare cheats), data in which White respondents, in particular, portray people of color in gross and dehumanizing ways, and data on the depth of violence in women's lives across race/ethnicity. (Fine and Weis 1999, 258-259)*

There is no one right way to manage this dilemma. If you do write up and present data which convey a negative impression, you may want to provide as much context as possible, so that your audiences can see the rationality for actions which they might otherwise consider deviant or unacceptable.[25]

(If your participants are involved in activities which are harmful distinct from simply stigmatizing or illegal, such as mistreatment of children, your dilemmas will be more intense. Be sure you are familiar with any laws which require you to report certain types of illegal activities, such as mandatory reporter regulations for people working with children.)

Maximalist Ethics

The core of what we call maximalist ethics—the responsibility of the researcher to not only avoid harm, but to actually do good—is endlessly debated among social scientists. Advocates of maximalist ethics invoke terms like "redistribution," and "social justice," while those of a more conservative bent tend to talk about "neutrality" and "objectivity."[26] Conservatives have argued that this activist approach to research politicizes what should be the disinterested pursuit of knowledge; while practitioners of socially engaged research respond that all knowledge creation is already inherently political, and that scholars must choose where they will situate themselves within the workings of power. These debates are especially keen in disciplines like sociology and anthropology, which have been connected to ethically dubious social projects such as colonialism or the Cold War in earlier decades. Historically, this maximalist approach has been associated with "studying down"—doing fieldwork among the oppressed or disenfranchised—but it is also compatible with "studying up"—working among the powerful with the intent of demystifying their power.

The question of whether fieldwork should be part of broader social change agendas is also particularly intense when researchers are in a privileged social position, whether by their own socioeconomic class or by the power and prestige of the institutions to which they are attached. Do such researchers have a particularly strong obligation to work against the same forces of inequality from which they may have benefited?[27] The authors of this book share a maximalist orientation, but we also recognize the unexpected problems that emerge when one tries to do good with one's research. Adopting a maximalist orientation to ethics undoubtedly imposes more responsibilities on the researcher than does the minimalist orientation, but it can also bring with it tremendous benefits in the form of satisfaction and a sense of agency for the researcher.

Researchers who believe that their foremost responsibility is to work for progressive changes face dilemmas in planning their fieldwork. For instance, they may be pulled between the kind of scholarship they find exciting and stimulating, such as "high theory," and the kind of scholarship they perceive as being of greatest political value. The research questions and areas of theory which grab and engage researchers may not be of great benefit, or even of interest, to the communities in which fieldwork is done. Participants generally prefer to hear that some concrete benefit is coming as a result of their involvement in research, rather than hearing that their experiences will break new ground in developing theory.

Researchers who adhere to a maximalist concept of ethics may also run up against the limits of scholarship. Very little academic research is actually world-altering, and the thought that one's work may end up in the form of journals or monographs of interest to a very small and specialized audience can be disheartening. Some researchers take comfort from the idea that letting people's stories be told, or giving them a forum to give voice to their experiences in the context of research, is in itself a positive contribution to the world, whether or not the act of "giving voice" leads to more material changes. For social scientists who adhere to this view, the production of new knowledge about disempowered communities is intrinsically liberatory. In some cases, your respondents may share this view of the emancipator power of simply taking part in research; in other cases they may not.

Lesson from the field:

For the privilege and opportunity to conduct research on an NGO's program, I often felt I owed the NGO the help they requested with extra jobs like writing questionnaires for other programs and statistical consulting. I tried to stay away from advising about substantive issues that would affect the program I was evaluating. I have always felt one ethical obligation in particular, which is to write a non-academic report aimed at the NGO's donors. I believe it is unfair to give the NGO an academic report that will not be read by donors or by other NGOs, although I have observed this to be common practice with many other NGO-academic relationships. (Paluck 2008, 15)

For researchers who want their work to transform the world as well as comment on it, concepts such as "empowerment," "participation," and "community" are key parts of planning and carrying out research. These concepts are embedded in a vast literature covering "action research." We will not review the definitions or the significance of these concepts here, but we do want to caution fieldworkers about the difficulties of translating these ideas into practice. If you are embarking on this type of research, it's wise to invest much time and reflection in advance of your fieldwork considering how these concepts will materialize in the nitty-gritty details of daily fieldwork. For instance, if you want your work to benefit "the community," who exactly is "the community?" How is it bounded? Does everyone in "the community" have the same interests, or the same concerns? Older people, to take one example, may have very different perceptions of their community's strengths and challenges than younger people. Whose interests will you be advancing? Similar careful thought should go into how you will operationalize other key concepts and ethical imperatives.

Institutional Ethics

Almost all institutions which sponsor research have bodies which must approve research plans before these can be carried out. Such bodies include institutional review boards (IRBs) in academic institutions, national research councils in many countries, or oversight committees for granting agencies. These bodies scrutinize research plans to ensure that they are compatible with the ethical guidelines set by the institution. You should know what institutional bodies need to approve your research plans, and get their formal approval before you begin activities which might be construed as research.[28] The line between preparing to do research and actually carrying it out is can be quite thin, especially if you're introducing yourself to people and settings which may be important in your research, by attending community events, for instance. However, it's important that you don't collect data which will be reproduced in your final product until you have whatever ethical clearances you need.

The use of ethics review committees in the social sciences is descended from their use in other forms of research, particularly medical research.[29] In medical research, the potential for bodily harm to participants is quite clear, and catastrophes like the Tuskegee experiment show why ethical review is needed. You may find ethical review unnecessarily restrictive, given that your research is not likely to kill or injure people, and a case can be made that the way ethical reviews are currently done is more appropriate for potentially physically dangerous research than for social sciences. Nonetheless, you'll still need ethics clearance for your work.

Institutional ethics review bodies are mainly concerned with two things—transparency and risk/benefit balance. The concern with transparency translates into being sure that everyone who is involved in the research understands that they are participating in a research project and agrees to take part. Rarely, ethical review bodies will approve research which is not transparent, in which research participants may not be aware they are being researched, or may actively be deceived. The main mechanism through which transparency is achieved is informed consent.[30] You should decide how best to inform the participants in your work about what the work involves, and how to ask them if they consent to being part of it. From an institutional perspective, the most important aspect of informed consent is proper documentation. (Such documentation can also be used to indemnify the institution, in the unlikely event that one of your participants decides to sue them over the consequences of participating in your research.) The formality of the consent process can also create tensions throughout the research process, depending on how the consent forms are interpreted by the researcher and participant.

Lesson from the field:

Before the study could be started, these steps were all taken

1. A four-page human subjects questionnaire was completed and submitted six weeks prior to beginning the study.

2. As part of the human subjects package, complete interview protocols were required for any interviews that were anticipated.

3. Copies of consent forms for the three student teachers were drafted and submitted.

4. All parties were briefed in detail.

5. All parties signed the consent forms.

Of course, none of this was difficult mechanically, and the point is not that paper work is a burden upon the researcher. But the emphasis on possible dangers to student teacher, cooperating teachers, or students never went away. The positive beginning that field workers hoped for was undermined. Members rarely understood the methodology when it was explained, and yet it had to be explained, since anonymity had to be preserved; when student teachers were told that they would be interviewed and possibly videotaped, one wanted to know:

Student teacher: "When will I be videotaped?"

Researcher: "We're not sure at this point."

Student teacher: "Why aren't you sure?"

Researcher: "It's too early in the study to know the exact day we'll want to tape you. Let's see how things progress-when you feel confident and have the class by yourself, probably."

Student teacher: "If you videotape and I look bad, or have a bad day, can I throw the tape away?"

Researcher: "I was hoping we could watch the tapes together so as to get some ideas of intentionality, purpose, etc."

Student teacher: "Well, don't you have to throw it away if I say so? It says right here on this form that you can't do anything I don't want you to do."

Researcher: "Yes, of course—we'll erase it if you wish." (sob). (DeVoss 1982, 41)

The usual way of documenting consent is through the consent form, which typically consists of a sheet with information about the project and then another sheet, to be signed by both the researcher and the participant, which states that the participant has freely chosen to take part in the project, that s/he knows s/he may withdraw from taking part at any point, and that s/he understands any possible risks or benefits to him or herself as a result of taking part. In some contexts, signing an informed consent form may not be appropriate, so you may have to think of other ways of documenting consent, such as audio- or videotaping participants' agreement. Some categories of people cannot give consent themselves, and a third party must give consent for them to participate. The definition of who can't consent on their own behalf varies from one institution to another, but always includes people under the legal age of adulthood, and usually involves people whose cognitive ability to understand the research is in doubt.

In addition to transparency, institutional ethics bodies are concerned with the balance between risk and benefit to participants in the research. In general, these bodies adhere strongly to the "do no harm" model of research, and want to be sure that you are not putting your participants at risk of any sort of negative outcome. If there is any risk, you must first ensure that you have plans for reducing this risk to the absolute minimum and/or that the potential benefit to the individual participant justifies the risk you are asking them to assume. For most social science research, the potential benefit to the individual participant is pretty small. In theory, your research may contribute to an improvement in the collective good somewhere down the line, but it's difficult to say that individual participants will benefit, unless they find the experience of being studied intrinsically interesting or entertaining.

Thus, in the (usual) absence of measurable individual benefits, your research planning should concentrate on minimizing possible risks to participants. For instance, if you want to interview people about some traumatic experience they have undergone, you can minimize the risk of re-traumatizing them by ensuring that you have arranged for skilled counselors to be available to them if they are distressed by talking about their experiences.

One of the most important ways of minimizing risk is through maximizing anonymity and confidentiality of your data, so that no one other than you (or your delegate) can ever link a specific participant to a specific element of data. Although anonymity and confidentiality are used interchangeably, they are two different things. Anonymity refers to the absence of any identifying material (for instance, interviewing people without getting their names or other details), while confidentiality refers to situations where identifying material exists, but is restricted. While anonymity offers better protection for your participants (especially if they are taking part in some illegal or stigmatized behavior or talking about very personal subjects), the importance of verifiability and validity in your data may mean that you will need to settle for confidentiality instead. Using a numerical code keyed to participants' names (and keeping the key separate from the data); transcribing all interview material or entering all survey data yourself; using pseudonyms in journal-keeping or observations; and keeping your data under physical lock and key are all good ways of increasing confidentiality.

Lesson from the field:

One of my students interviewed survivors of trauma for her dissertation. One man she interviewed had been a political prisoner and had been tortured by the government of his home country. Although the consent letter stipulated that identities would be kept confidential by using pseudonyms in the presentation of the research, this man wanted his real name and country to be used. He argued that he did not want to collude in silence around this country's practice of torture, and that it was important to use his own name to demonstrate that he hadn't been cowed by what he had experienced. The university

> *ethics committee however would not permit this. They argued that this man had no way of knowing what future consequences might arise from having his name publicly attached to these allegations against his country, and that by requiring him to be "pseudonymized", they were protecting him against himself.*

Thus far our discussions about ethics have centered around possibilities and potential for harm and benefits of the research for the participant. It is also important to ensure that the researcher's safety is considered and that potential harm is minimized.[31] This could mean having safety measures in place. This could mean arranging to call a colleague or friend after an interview, especially if you are interviewing at someone else's home. It might also mean careful consideration of location of research to balance out potential harms and benefits.

Regardless of which approach to research ethics you adhere to, it is important to think through ethical implications of your work and to seek advice from experienced researchers when you are presented with ethical dilemmas (because the will likely arise). These dilemmas and questions are a continuous part of the research process and are not limited to considerations while drafting the ethical protocol required by the institutional review board.

Chapter 7

Concluding Thoughts

Now that you've reached the end of this book, the most important thing to remember is that nothing we've said here should be taken as prescriptive, or as a reliable prediction of how your own fieldwork will unfold. Research in the field, whatever your field may be, is dynamic and ever changing, making it difficult to provide novice researchers with detailed guidelines or "rules" to follow. What works in one setting, or for one project, or researcher may not work on another day or in another situation. Researchers must therefore be skilled improvisers, able to adapt to their field situations and make "game time" decisions that may shape their project in drastic ways. At the same time, researchers must temper their flexibility with commitment to the core concerns that animate their research project, whether these concerns are empowering people to improve their lives, increasing empirical knowledge about a social phenomenon, advancing theory, or answering a pressing policy question. In this book, we have given you skills and advice to help you balance the improvisational demands of fieldwork with the goals of your project.

Several overarching themes run through the topics covered in this book.

Expect the Unexpected

Even the best most thought out and developed research designs will inevitably come across unexpected events, challenges and opportunities. These could be in the form of challenges to the research design (difficulties that make it hard to implement the research design as is), as ethical dilemmas, or in the form of assumptions made by the participants that challenge the researcher's perspective of his or her research, position or identity. Meeting the unexpected can be one of the great parts of fieldwork, and research is often enriched by fortuitous opportunities and unforeseen possibilities which emerge in the course of fieldwork. However, in order to minimize potential negative consequences from these unexpected events, we encourage you to do two things:

1. Begin with a solid plan. This may seem to run counter to our advice about the improvisational nature of fieldwork, but starting with a solid plan ensures that the researcher is well grounded in what they see as the broad research goals and the reasons behind those goals. These goals might have to do with the research questions and understanding a particular topic (in which case the methods may be open for negotiation as long as the focus of the research remains similar). Perhaps the goals of the project have to do with improving the lives of the community members (in which case being flexible to their needs is paramount), or maybe the project was designed to give the researcher experience with a particular method or technique (in which case the topic may be open to negotiation). Having a firm understanding of why the research is taking place will help you decide which challenges/road blocks are worth trying to push through and when to bend or amend the research design protocol. Without a solid plan a researcher might be tempted to "go where the wind blows" and end up with a project that lacks cohesion or sense of direction, or might try to "stick to the plan" in ways that are too rigid and might not be important to the overall goal of the project.

2. To borrow from Janice Morse, it is always good to perform an "armchair walkthrough," in which the researcher sits down and systematically visualizes all aspects of their project. They can imagine going to their field site, connecting with people, collecting data, dealing with ethical issues, and even think through and anticipate some challenges that may arise due to identity characteristics (for example what would it be like for an adoptive parent to conduct research with adults who were adopted as children). The point again is not to anticipate everything that might happen, but to be as prepared as possible and (perhaps more importantly) to begin to identify the assumptions and expectations that you are bringing into the research, such as what you expect your participants to be like, to do, or how you anticipate people will react to your project. This is also an opportunity to think about how the researcher expects their identity and personal characteristics to influence the field experience. By identifying the assumptions we have when we enter the field we will be better prepared to deal with challenges to those assumptions and will be quicker to recognize when those assumptions are incorrect.

Make Game Time Decisions

In addition to expecting to be surprised and challenged, it is also important to be prepared to make decisions that may change the course of your field work, and even the focus of your project. The ability to make (good) decisions in the moment will also depend on good planning. Depending on where and how the project is being conducted it might not be possible for graduate students to contact their supervisor in a timely manner, and they may have to be prepared to make decisions without the benefit of the advice of their supervisor. It is important to talk with supervisors, colleagues and other stakeholders before the start of the project to ensure that everyone is on the same page regarding the goals of the project, and to confirm that you as the researcher will be able to exercise your own discretion in the field to change or alter aspects of the research.

Yet, making good decisions is not just about being prepared and understanding the project, it also takes confidence. Prior to beginning the fieldwork ensure you are confident in your understanding of the project, the methods and yourself as a researcher. This confidence will help you make better decisions. Remember that even a less than ideal decision is better than failing to make a decision and ending up with a hodge podge of this and that. Qualitative researchers often use memoing and/or journaling to record impressions of the field and decisions they make while in the field. It is important to record in here the reasons behind the decisions you made and the circumstances behind those decisions. These will help later when it comes to the analysis of your data, so that you can explain to yourself and to others why you made the choices that you did.

Think Reflexively

Throughout the research process it is important to think about the process and how the research is succeeding, where the fieldwork could improve and how your role as a researcher is developing. Qualitative researchers use reflexivity to varying degrees. At minimum, it is important to continuously think through how the project is going and how the goals of the project are being achieved, rather than simply plowing ahead with a pre-set agenda. For projects using maximalist ethics it might be beneficial to have casual conversations with key community members to get a sense of how the research is impacting the community and if there are other needs that might require attention.

Enjoy the Process

Fieldwork is not always fun. However, it can provide you with unparalleled opportunities to develop new skills, visit places which might otherwise have been geographically or socially inaccessible, create some positive change for the world, and bring home your own collection of tales from the field. If you're alert to the enjoyment and stimulation fieldwork affords, its stresses and challenges will pale in comparison.

Notes

Chapter 1

1. Gupta and Ferguson's (1997) edited text provides numerous discussions about the field as it applies to anthropological work.

2. Tedlock (2000) provides a lovely brief history of ethnography which describes the development of thinking around fieldwork.

3. For a theoretical discussion on the nature of the field (and the changes of definition of the field over the last few decades) see Amit (2000), particularly the introduction. and Hume and Mulcock (2004).

4. Kurotani (2004) has a particularly interesting discussion of multi-sited research.

5. Ruhleder (2000) discusses the challenges of fieldwork in the virtual world.

6. See Eisenhart (2001) for a succinct review of the changing conceptualization of culture in social science research.

7. For a summary of the history of this debate see Naples (1996). For more recent discussions of these issues and a questioning of the insider/outsider distinction see Lundy (2006), Watts (2007).
8. Adler and Adler (1987) provide an outline of different relationships that researchers can have with those in their field site. For a more recent analysis of these roles see Acker (2000), Kanuha (2000), Mullings (1999), and Dwyer and Buckle (2009).

Chapter 2

9. For further discussion of entry into the field see Bailey (1996), Jorgensen (1989), and Lofland and Lofland (1995).
10. For an in depth discussion of the field see Amit (2000).
11. See Sandelowski (1995) for a quick primer on determining appropriate sample sizes in qualitative research.
12. Kurotani (2004) provides a nice introduction to the differences between multi-sited research and more traditional single-sited research.
13. See Ruhleder (2000) for an in depth discussion on qualitative field work in virtual communities.

Chapter 3

14. For more in depth exploration of insider and outsider debates see Acer (2000), Adler and Adler (1987), Dwyer and Buckle (2009), Kanuha (2000), and Mullings (1999).

Chapter 4

15. See Coffey (1999) for an in depth examination of issues of identity as they relate to fieldwork. Lewing and Leap (1996) produced an edited text with a discussion about experiences of Lesbian and Gay fieldworkers.

16. See Telfer (2004) for an account of being both insider and outsider in a community of adoptive parents.
17. See Elwood and Martin (2000) for a discussion of the ways in which the physical spaces in which interviews take place embody the different social locations of research and participant.

Chapter 5

18. See Charmaz (2000) for a description of how grounded theory has been used within multiple research paradigms.
19. See Sanjek (1990) and Wolfinger (2002) for detailed discussions of fieldnotes, their purpose and how to collect them.

Chapter 6

20. See Clark and Scharf (2007) on inadvertent harm to participants.
21. See Del Monte (2010) for discussion of another aspect of "fitting in"—working in teams with differing personal and professional agendas.
22. See Wolcott (2002) for an account of a relationship with a long-term research participant which ended badly.
23. See the contributors to Josselson (1996) on the ethical dilemmas posed by fieldwork which may cause distress to others.
24. See Sanjak (2004) for a discussion of the repercussions of research on political change in a New York neighborhood following the author's publication of his findings.
25. See Calvey (2008) for a discussion of "situated ethics" and researchers' responses to observing illegal and potentially unethical activities. See also Vanderstaay (2005) for more on the dilemmas raised by unethical activities perpetrated by informants.

26. See Bourgois (1990) for a classic statement of researchers' responsibility to do good rather than merely observing. For more recent consideration of researchers' role in generating empowerment and social justice see Wood (2006), Harrowing et al. (2010), and Scheyvens and Leslie (2010).

27. See Wong (1998) for reflection on how differences in gender, race and class may have shaped research with low-income women of color.

28. See Johnson (2008) for an account of the difficulties of obtaining formal institutional ethics approval for field research on sensitive topics involving sexuality.

29. For a glimpse of how clinicians and medical scientists view ethics in research, see Hoeyer et al. (2000) and Ladd et al. (2009).

30. For an argument that the notion of informed consent is culturally-specific and not universally transferrable, see Marzano (2007).

31. See Kovats-Bernat (2002) for a practical approach to minimizing danger to oneself when conducting research in unsafe environments.

References

Acker, S. 2001. In/out/side: Positioning the researcher in feminist qualitative research. *Resources for Feminist Research* 28(3/4): 153.

Adler, P., and P. Adler. 1987. *Membership Roles in Field Research.* Newbury Park, CA: Sage Publications.

Amit, V. 2000. *Constructing the Field: Ethnographic Fieldwork in the Contemporary World.* New York: Routledge.

Ayi, B., S. Harrell, and M. Lunzy. 2007. *Fieldwork Connections: The Fabric of Ethnographic Collaboration in China and America.* Seattle, WA: University of Washington.

Bailey, C. A. 1996. A Guide to Field Research. Thousand Oaks, CA: Sage Publications.

Bourgois, P. 1990. Confronting anthropological ethics: Ethnographic lessons from Central America. *Journal of Peace Research* 27(1): 43-54.

Chapman, R., and J. Berggren. 2004. Radical contextualization: Contributions to an anthropology of racial/ethnic health disparities. *Health: An Interdisciplinary Journal for the Social Study of Health, Illness and Medicine* 9(2):145-167.

Charmaz, K. 2000. Grounded theory: Objectivist and constructivist methods. In N. K. Denzin and Y. S. Lincoln, eds. *Handbook of Qualitative Research*. 509-534.

Clark, C. 2007. The dark side of the truth(s): Ethical dilemmas in researching the personal. *Qualitative Inquiry* 13 (3): 399-416.

Coffey, A. 1999. *The Ethnographic Self: Fieldwork and the Representation of Identity*. London: Sage Publications.

DeVoss, G., N. Zimpher, and N. Nott. 1990. Ethics in field work research: A case study. *The Urban Review* 14(1): 35-46.

Drybread, K. 2006. Sleeping with one eye open: The perils of fieldwork in a Brazilian juvenile prison. In A. Gardner and D. M. Hoffman, eds. *Dispatches from the Field: Neophyte Ethnographers in a Changing World*. Long Grove, IL: Waveland Press. 33-52.

Dwyer, S. C., and J. L. Buckle. 2009. The space between: On being an insider-outsider in qualitative research. *International Journal of Qualitative Methods* 8(1): 54-63.

Eisenhart, M. 2001. Changing conceptions of culture and ethnographic methodology: Recent thematic shifts and their implications for research on teaching. In V. Richardson, ed. *Handbook of Research on Teaching, 4th Edition*. Washington, DC: American Educational Research Association. 209-225.

Elwood, S.A., and D.G. Martin. 2000. "Placing" interviews: Location and scales of power in qualitative research. *The Professional Geographer* 52(4): 649-657.

Fadzillah, I. 2004. Going beyond "the West" and "the rest": Conducting non-Western and non-native ethnography in Northern Thailand. In L. Hume and J. Mulcock, eds. *Anthropologists in the Field: Cases in Participant Observation*. NY, NY: Columbia University Press. 32-45.

Forsey, M. 2004. "He's not a spy; he's one of us": Ethnographic positioning in a middle-class setting. In L. Hume and J.

Mulcock, eds. *Anthropologists in the Field: Cases in Participant Observation.* NY, NY: Columbia University Press. 32-45.

Gupta, A., and J. Ferguson. 1997. *Anthropological Locations: Boundaries and Grounds of Field Science.* Berkeley, CA: University of California Press.

Harrowing, J., et al. 2010. Culture, community and context: Ethical considerations for global nursing research. *International Nursing Review* 57(1): 70-77.

Hoeyer, K., L. Dahlager, and N. Lynoe. 2005. Conflicting notions of research ethics: The mutually challenging traditions of social scientists and medical researchers. *Social Science and Medicine* 61(8): 174-179.

Irwin, K. 2006. Into the dark heart of ethnography: The lived ethics and inequality of intimate field relationships. *Qualitative Sociology* 29(2): 155-175.

Hume, L., and J. Mulcock. 2004. *Anthropologists in the Field: Cases in Participant Observation.* New York: Columbia University Press.

Johnson, T. 2008. Qualitative research in question: A narrative account of disciplinary power with/in the IRB. *Qualitative Inquiry* 14(8): 212-232.

Jorgensen, D. L. 1989. *Participant Observation: A Methodology of Human Studies.* Newbury Park, CA: Sage Publications.

Kanuha, V. K. 2000. "Being" native versus "going native": Conducting social work research as an insider. *Social Work* 45(5): 439-447.

Kelly, P. 2004. Awkward intimacies: Prostitution, politics and fieldwork in urban Mexico. In L. Hume and J. Mulcock, eds. *Anthropologists in the Field: Cases in Participant Observation.* NY, NY: Columbia University Press. 3-17.

Kovats-Bernat, J. C. 2002. Negotiating dangerous fields: Pragmatic strategies for fieldwork amid violence and terror. *American Anthropologist* 104(1): 208-222.

Kurotani, S. 2004. Multi-sited transnational ethnography and the shifting construction of fieldwork. In L. Hume and J. Mulcock, eds. *Anthropologists in the Field: Cases in Participant Observation*. New York, NY: Columbia University Press. 201-215.

Ladd, J.M.,et al. 2009. The hows and whys of research: Life scientists' views of accountability. *Journal of Medical Ethics* 35 (12): 762-767.

Leslie, H., and D. Storey. 2003. Practical issues. In R. Scheyvens and D. Storey, eds. *Development Fieldswork: A Practical Guide*. London: Sage. 77-96.

Lewin, E., and W.L. Leap. 1996. *Out in the Field: Reflections of Lesbian and Gay Anthropologists*. Urbana, IL: University of Illinois Press.

Lofland, J., and L.H. Lofland. 1995. *Analyzing Social Settings: A Guide to Qualitative Observation and Analysis*. Belmont, CA: Wadsworth.

Lozanski, K., and M. Beres. 2007. Temporary transience and qualitative research: Methodological lessons from fieldwork with independent travelers and seasonal workers. *International Journal of Qualitative Methods* 6(2): Article 8. Retrieved 10 October 2007 from http://www.ualberta.ca/~iiqm/backissues/6_2/lozanski.pdf.

Lundy, P., and M. McGovern. 2006. Participation, truth and partiality: Participatory action research in northern Ireland. *Sociology* 40 (1): 71-88.

Maticka-Tyndale, E., E.S. Herold, and M. Oppermann. 2003. Casual sex among Australian schoolies. *Journal of Sex Research* 40: 158-160.

Marzano, M. 2007. Informed consent, deception and research freedom in qualitative research: A cross-cultural comparison. *Qualitative Inquiry* 13: 417-436.

Mullings, B. 1999. Insider or outsider, both or neither: Some dilemmas of interviewing in a cross-cultural setting. *Geoform* 30: 337-350.

Murray, W. E., and J. Overton. 2003. Designing development research. In R. Scheyvens and D. Storey, eds. *Development Fieldswork: A Practical Guide*. London: Sage. 17-36.

Naples, N. A. 1996. A feminist revisiting of the insider/outsider debate: The "outsider phenomenon" in rural Iowa. *Qualitative Sociology* 19: 83-106.

Ronai, C. R. 1992. The reflexive self through narrative: A night in the life of an erotic dancer/researcher. In C.E. and M.G. Flaherty, eds. *Investigating Subjectivity: Research on Lived Experience*. Newbury Park, CA: Sage Publications. 102-124.

Paluck, E.L. 2007. Reducing Intergroup Prejudice and Conflict with the Media: A Field Experiment in Rwanda. Yale University.

Pierce, J. 1995. *Gender Trials: EmotionalLives in Contemporary Law Firms*. Berkeley, CA: University of California Press.

Ruhleder, K. 2000. The virtual ethnographer: Fieldwork in distributed electronic environments. *Field Methods* 12: 3-17.

Sandelowski, M. 1995. Sample size in qualitative research. *Research in Nursing and Health* 18: 179-183.

Sandstrom, A. 2006. The wave: Fieldwork and friendship in Northern Veracruz, Mexico. In B. T. Grindal and F. A. Salamone, eds. *Bridges to Humanity: Narratives on Fieldwork and Friendship, 2nd ed*. Long Grove, IL: Waveland Press. 7-27.

Sanjek, R. 1990. *Fieldnotes: The Makings of Anthropology*. Ithica, NY: Cornell University Press.

Scheyvens, R., and H. Leslie. 2000. Gender, ethics and empowerment: Dilemmas of development fieldwork. *Women's Studies International Forum* 23(1): 119-130.

Tedlock, B. 2000. Ethnography and ethnographic representation. In N. K. Denzin and Y. S. Lincoln, eds. *Handbook of Qualitative Research (2nd Edition)*. Thousand Oaks, CA: Sage Publications. 455-486.

Telfer, J. 2004. Dissent and consent: Negotiating the adoption triangle. In L. Hume and J. Mulcock, eds. *Anthropologists in the Field: Cases in Participant Observation*. NY: Columbia University Press. 71-81.

Vanderstaay, S. 2010. One hundred dollars and a dead man: Ethical decision making in ethnographic research. *Journal of Contemporary Ethnography* 34(4): 371-409.

Watts, J. 2007. The outsider within: Dilemmas of feminist research within a culture of resistance. *Qualitative Sociology* 6(3): 385-402.

Wolfinger, N. H. 2002. On writing fieldnotes: Collection strategies and background expectancies. *Qualitative Research* 2: 85-95.

Wolcott, H. F. 2002. *Sneaky Kid and Its Aftermath: Ethics and Intimacy in Fieldwork*. Lanham, MD: Alta Mira Press.

Wong, L.M. 1998. The ethics of rapport: Institutional safeguards, resistance and betrayal. *Qualitative Inquiry* 4(2)1: 178-199.

Wood, E.J. 2006. The ethical challenges of field research in conflict zones. *Qualitative Sociology* 29(3): 373-386.

Index

Aboriginal communities of Canada, 26–27
Academic research, concept of, 33–34
Accountability for field researcher, 47–49
Action-research, 9–10
Anonymity in data collection, 105–106
Armchair walkthrough, 109
Asymmetries of power, 40–42

Back-translation surveys, 45
Boundaries
  of field researcher, 38
  of fieldwork, 20–22

Chapman, Rachel, 20–21
Chirungu, 86–87
Chivanhu, 86–87
Commitments, ongoing, 54–56
Community, researcher connections in, 35–37
Community investment
  during fieldwork, 26
  insider researcher and, 37–39
  ongoing, 54–56
  outsider researcher and, 32–33
Confidentiality in data collection, 105–106

Consent process, 102–104
Contributors, acknowledging, 30
Data collection
  anonymity in, 105–106
  confidentiality in, 105–106
  empirical question in, 75–76
  failures in, 73
  field location and, 19
  flexibility in, 75
  language and, 19–20
  loyalty to participants vs. data, 97–98
  organizing for, 30
  pilot study and, 79
  places for, 16–20
  pre-fieldwork preparation, 77–78
  preparatory work, 76–79, 101
  qualitative methods for, 16–17
  quantitative methods for, 16
  reflexivity, 75
  research plans, 74
  roadblocks in. *See* roadblocks
  saturation, 21–22
  stakeholders in, 18
  time and space boundaries of, 20–22
  transparencies in, 95
  See also fieldwork

123

Deep acting, 35
Disenfranchised groups, 27
"Do no harm" model of research, 104
Embodiment, 65
Empirical question, 75–76
Ethics
  anonymity in data collection and, 105–106
  confidentiality in data collection and, 105–106
  cost of fitting in, 92
  defined, 91
  informed consent and, 102–104
  institutional ethics, 101–105
  maximalist ethics, 98–101
  minimalist ethics, 92–98
  offending existing norms, 92–93
  participant benefits from research, 99
  participant's psychological well-being and, 95–97
  participant's reputation and, 97–98
  participants' resources and, 93–94
  risk/benefit balance in, 104–106
  time exploitation and, 94–95
  transparency, 95, 102
Ethics review committees, 101–102
Ethnic identity, 62–63
Ethnography, 9
Euphemisms. *See* language and data collection
Events, unexpected, 108–109

Field conditions, roadblocks in, 84–85
Field location, 19
Field personality, 34–35
Field researcher
  accountability as, 47–49
  awkward situations for, 68–69
  boundaries of, 38
  competing goals with participants, 66–68
  conflicting views with participants, 69–71
  decision-making for, 109–110
  forming alliances with participants, 68–69
  identities of, 62–64, 71–72
  relationship between participants and, 58–60
  role of, 58–60
  See insider researcher; outsider researcher; researcher identity
Fieldwork
  acclimatize to, 23–24
  acknowledging contributors, 30
  action-research, 9–10
  boundaries of, 20–22
  building relationships, 25
  decision-making, 109–110
  defined, 9–10
  disenfranchised groups and, 27
  ending, 29–30
  ethical issues in, 65–66
  ethnography, 9
  formal entry into, 27–28
  geographic, 10–11
  interpersonal situations in. *See* interpersonal situations
  interviews and focus groups, 10
  investing in community during, 25–26
  multi-sited research, 10–11, 22
  planning the research, 16–20, 108–109
  self-reliance in the field, 78–79
  sensitive topics and, 27, 95–96
  social, 11–12
  virtual research, 11, 22–23
  volunteering during, 25–26
  See also data collection; field researcher
Fieldwork journal, 90
Flexibility, 75

Gathering data. *See* data collection
Gender, 60–61
Geographic fieldwork, 10–11

Hawthorne effect, 88
Hierarchical relationships
  accountability and, 47–49
  asymmetries of power, 40–42
  defined, 39–40
  between researcher and RA, 42–46

Identity. *See* researcher identity
Inductive methodologies, 85–86

Informed consent, 102–104
Insider researcher, 11–12, 37–39, 58–60
Institutional ethics, 101–105
Institutional review boards (IRBs), 101
Internet access, 79
Interpersonal situations
 invitations, 52–54
 money, 49–51
 ongoing community investment, 54–56
 sexual relationships, 51–52
Invitations during fieldwork, 52–54

Jargon. *See* language and data collection
Justice, redistributive, 54–55

Language and data collection, 19–20
Lozanski, Kristin, 29

Maximalist ethics, 98–101
Medical research, 101
Methodology roadblocks, 83–84
Minimalist ethics
 offending existing norms, 92–93
 participant's psychological well-being and, 95–97
 participant's reputation and, 97–98
 participants' resources and, 93–94
 time exploitation and, 94–95
Money, lending and borrowing, 49–51
Multi-sited research, 10–11, 22

National research councils, 101

Outsider researcher
 asking questions, 35
 conforming to stereotypes, 34
 connections in community, 35–37
 deep acting for, 35
 defined, 11–12
 personality of, 34–35
 relationship between participants and, 58–60
 shaping community expectations, 32–33
 starting out as, 32
Oversight committees, 101

Participants
 benefits from research, 99
 competing goals with researcher, 66–68
 conflicting views with researcher, 69–71
 demand on resources, 93–94
 forming alliances with researcher, 68–69
 informed consent of, 102–104
 loyalty to, 97–98
 offending, 92–93
 psychological well-being of, 95–97
 relationship between field researcher and, 58–60
 reputation of, 97–98
 resources of, 93–94
 risk/benefit balance to, 104–106
 time exploitation and, 94–95
Personality, field, 34–35
Pierce, Jennifer, 60–61
Pilot study, 79
Power asymmetries, 40–42
Pre-fieldwork preparation, 77–78

Qualitative methods, 16–17
Quantitative methods, 16

RA. *See* research assistant (RA)
Race, 60–61
Reciprocity, 54–55
Redistributive justice, 54–55
Reflexivity, 75
Relationships. *See* hierarchical relationships
Religious affiliation, 69
Research assistant (RA)
 back-translation, 45
 debriefing, 45–46
 as friend, 46–47
 role of, 42–43
 role-playing with, 45
 training and dialogue, 44
Research ethics. *See* ethics
Research process
 enjoyment during, 110–111
 planning, 16–20
 thinking reflexively, 110
 unexpected events, 108–109

Researcher. *See* field researcher; researcher identity
Researcher identity
  assigned identities, 62–64
  balancing identities, 64–66
  competing goals of participants and, 66–68
  conflicting views with participants 69–71
  dealing with stakeholders, 66–68
  ethical issues, 65–66
  forming alliances with participants 68–69
  impact on research, 59
  relationship between participants and, 58–60
  shaping the research project, 71–72
  social markers, 60–61
  See also insider researcher; outsider researcher
Risk/benefit balance, 104–106
Roadblocks
  biased information, 88–89
  blocked access to data, 81–82
  distorted data collection method, 88–89
  field conditions, 84–85
  lack of access to data, 81–82
  methodology, 83–84
  sensitive topics, 80
  theories in advance of data, 85–87
  unanswerable research questions, 79–80
Role-playing with RAs, 45

Safe space for researcher, 70–71
Saturation, 21–22
Self-reliance in the field, 78–79
Sensitive subject matter, 27, 80, 95–96
Sexual relationships during fieldwork, 51–52
Slang. *See* language and data collection
Social fieldwork, 11–12
Social markers, 60–61
Space boundaries of data collection, 20–22
Stakeholders, 18, 66–68
Stereotypes, 34
Studying down, 99
Studying up, 99
Surveys, 45

Taboo subject matter, 80
Telfer, David, 22
Telfer, Jon, 17–18
Thompson, Guy, 34
Time, 20–22, 94–95
Training and dialogue with RAs, 44
Transparency, 95, 102

Unexpected events during research, 108–109

Virtual research, 11, 22–23
Volunteer efforts during fieldwork, 25–26

About the Authors

Amy Kaler is an associate professor in the Department of Sociology and the School of Public Health at the University of Alberta. She studies the institutional contexts of reproductive and sexual health, with emphasis on birth control and sexually transmitted diseases. Her research focuses on southern and eastern Africa and western Canada. She is the author of *Running After Pills: Politics, Gender and Contraception in Colonial Zimbabwe* and co-editor of *The Gendered Society Reader* (Canadian edition). She has also published extensively in leading journals in sociology, history, public health, and gender studies.

Melanie Beres is a lecturer in the Department of Anthropology, Gender and Sociology at the University of Otago, New Zealand. She has conducted field research in Canada and New Zealand. To date, her "field" has remained relatively close to home, including research with transient youth in a small resort community in the Canadian Rockies. She has several previous publications and conference papers based on fieldwork research and about fieldwork, with a focus on research with transient populations. Currently she teaches research methods, theories of social power and social inequality. Her current research projects are focused on exploring power in intimate relationships in local and international contexts.